THE TRAIL TO LOVE
COLLABORATIVE ATTACHMENT SYSTEMS THERAPY

KYLE N. WEIR, PHD, LMFT
CALIFORNIA STATE UNIVERSITY - FRESNO
WORKBOOK 2 FOR COUPLES

Copyright © 2021 by Kyle N. Weir, PhD, LMFT

Published by Finegold Creek Press, LLC

P.O. Box 1272

Washington, UT 84780

All rights reserved.

No part of this book may be reproduced in any form or by any electronic or mechanical means, including information storage and retrieval systems, without written permission from the author, except for the use of brief quotations in a book review.

The information in this book is for informational and educational purposes and is not intended to be a substitute for professional medical or therapeutic advice, diagnosis, or treatment.

*For my wife, Allison -
Who's been with me on every step
along the TRAIL to Love.*

CONTENTS

The TRAIL to Love	vii
1. Chapter One - Trust	1
2. Chapter Two - Regard	17
3. Chapter 3 - Attachment: Applied	39
4. Chapter Four - Intimacy	53
5. Chapter Five - Love	65
Continuing Therapy with Collaborative Attachment Systems Therapy	77
Notes	81
About the Author	85

THE TRAIL TO LOVE

Workbook 2 for Couples

The TRAIL to Love

- Systems
- Attachment
- Collaborative

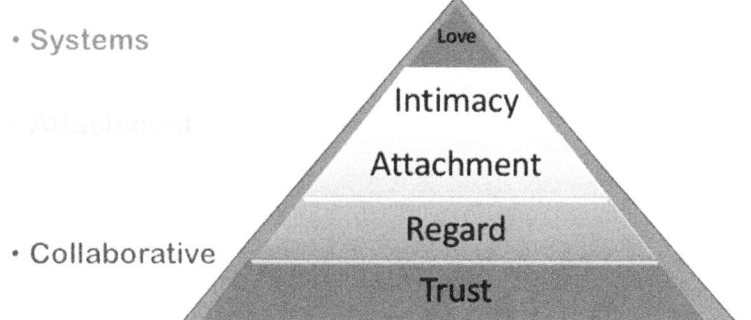

CHAPTER ONE - TRUST

*H*ow does a person initially develop trust in another person? In therapy sessions with couples, I often deal with the corollary question: how does a person rebuild trust after it has been lost through a betrayal or breach of trust? Trust is the essence of building or rebuilding a relationship. Without trust, the remainder of the TRAIL to Love (regard, attachment, intimacy, and love) cannot emerge in new relationships nor can they long endure in a relationship that is being repaired and rebuilt.

One of my graduate school supervisors was Marcia Lasswell, a Past-President of the American Association for Marriage and Family Therapists (AAMFT). In her sweet Oklahoma-born accent, she would often say, "Building trust is simple. Step one, never do anything your spouse wouldn't approve of. Step two, when you do (meaning do something they wouldn't approve of), tell them immediately." I have always loved that folksy wisdom that seemed to exude from her in a loving, gentle way – stating things in the way a kind grandma would say something who is willing to "tell it to you straight." Trust is built by collaborating with your partner about what actions are acceptable and not acceptable in the relationship. When there is an instance where one or the other falls short of the expected standard (because we are all human and make mistakes), be immediately forthcoming and transparent as you strive to repair the relationship breach and change to conform to the expectation. But that practical advice about building trust is often easier said than done. Why? The answer is twofold. One, people often are not trustworthy nor do they have integrity – that has to change to forge trust. Secondly, building trust takes a measure of vulnerability. That often includes exploring and addressing painful emotions, resentments, memories, and prior attachment patterns which can get in the way of being vulnerable enough to form or reform trust.

Often, I work with couples where some type of addiction is either present or is part of their recent past. Naturally, the non-addicted partner loses trust in their addicted spouse or companion. One alumni of our addiction treatment program often tells the story of meeting with his accountability partner (similar to a sponsor or mentor in his recovery) and asking, "How can I get my partner to trust me?" The sponsor said, "You can't. You can only *be* trustworthy." Being trustworthy and never lying to his wife became his bottom line key to success in recovery.

A partner cannot trust someone who isn't trustworthy. That is just a crazy-making process for them. It is traumatizing to repeatedly place your trust in someone who will repeatedly hurt and violate that trust over and over again. So, the first key to building or rebuilding trust is that untrustworthy behaviors, action tendencies, words, and deeds have to be discontinued.

Sometimes a couple may not agree on what is acceptable or not acceptable behavior. That is a little more complicated, but not insurmountable. Each partner must be willing to listen to the other persons reasons and feelings, take time to consider all the aspects, and then use the conflict resolution style of collaborating (or at the least compromise) to come to agreement. Dr. Ivan Boszormenyi-Nagy described the necessary type of conversation as a "genuine dialogue among the family members regarding important issues of family life, done in a manner which recognizes differences and conflicts as valuable reconcilable ingredients, rather than obstacles to relating and growth."[1] What are the current "obstacles" or barriers to trust in your relationship? How can you change them from obstacles into "reconcilable ingredients" for relating better to each other, growing together, and trusting more?

Partner 1:
_____
_____
_____

Partner 2:
_____
_____
_____

BECOMING **Trustworthy**

Dr. Gottman highlights five key components of a trustworthy person.[2] These five components of trustworthiness can also be used by a spouse or partner to determine the level of trustworthiness they see in their partner.

1. **Honesty** – the person does not lie or deceive. They do not want deception in any context – either by lies of commission or lies of omission – to erode the trust their partner has in them.
2. **Transparency** – the person is an open book. While it can be tempting to try to hide an uncomfortable truth from another, the person has the character that being honest and forthright is better than secret-keeping regardless of the rationalizations others might use to justify lying and secrecy in the same scenario. In our modern times of the digital age, couples need to be able to access each other's technology (smartphones, tablets, emails, social media, and other digital devices) except in the portions where legally protected information exists (such as work files, confidential patient records, matters of national security,

3. **Accountability** – the person does what he or she says or promises they would do, and they are willing to provide evidence or proof of it. As President Ronald Reagan famously stated about his approach to the former Soviet Union, you must "trust, but verify."[3] A trustworthy person is accountable to their partner for their actions.
4. **Ethics** – the person has a good set of moral or ethical standards that the other partner agrees with. The partner has "witnessed this person having consistent standards of just and fair conduct with others."[4]
5. **Alliance** – the person is "totally on your side."[5] They are loyal and have your best interests at heart, without ulterior or selfish motives. They are willing to work, sacrifice, and cooperate for your good and the good of the relationship.

Throughout his book, *The Science of Trust*, Gottman describes trust as something that evolves or ripens from predictable, dependable, reliable interactions.[6] It involves loyalty vs. betrayal.[7] It involves an "optimal" balance of power that seems fair – at least in the sense of people getting their needs met.[8] Trust stems from mutual support and a "willingness to put one's self at risk" or be vulnerable by "sacrificing present rewards for future gains."[9] It leads to overall positive feelings toward one another (what Gottman calls "positive sentiment override").[10] But mostly, trust is built through emotional attunement – moments where one has a bid for connection and the other is willing to "be there" for them.[11] "Happy couples" talk about "feelings" and "needs"[12] in a gentle way (sounds a lot like collaboration), but more than talk, they've learned to "be there"[13] for each other.

GOTTMAN RECOGNIZES that trusting relationships are not a zero-sum game. You can both win – it doesn't have to be a win/lose scenario. In fact, you should usually strive for a win/win outcome in your relationship. He talks about trust in terms of cooperation (work or effort on your partner's behalf) without sacrificing one's own needs (basically describing collaboration – high assertiveness of one's own needs and one's high cooperation to meet partner's needs):

> "(Trust) reflects cooperation with one's partner's interests in mind, probably important in any lasting relationship. Notice also that I am *not* mentioning consideration for one person's gains over and above consideration for the other partner's gains. Trust, in this view, does not require sacrifice of one's own interests in the conflict for the partner's interests or gains."[14]

WHICH OF THE five components of trustworthiness (honesty, transparency, accountability, ethics, and alliance) do you feel you need to improve on so that your partner can trust you more?

Partner 1:
_____
_____
_____

Partner 2:
_____
_____
_____

What components of trustworthiness do you need your partner to improve on to be able to trust him or her more?

Partner 1:
_____
_____
_____

Partner 2:
_____
_____
_____

...

TRUST AS A COLLABORATIVE BALANCE OF LOYALTIES, Needs, and Sacrifices

From the descriptions of trust described by Dr. Gottman, we see trust as an activating mechanism that balances both assertiveness of one's own needs with cooperation in meeting a partner's interests – the quintessential definition of collaboration. Similarly, Dr. Ivan Boszormenyi-Nagy viewed trust as balance of ethics (which he described as being true to one's self) with loyalties (which he described as fulfilling our obligations to others). The balance of trust is structured in a way that neither sacrifices one's self needs too much (though some sacrifice is necessary for cooperation at times) nor shirks loyalty obligations to others. He also spoke of balancing the needs of the individual with the needs of the multi-person family system as a whole,[15] and saw family life as an unending process of "give and take" where the interactions generally met the fair and equitable needs of all. Thus, the sacrifices one makes for their partner or their entire family system highlight the root meaning of the word sacrifice – to make sacred. As each family member makes sacrifices for the greater good of each other in a give and take reciprocity, a sacred bond of trust forms and deepens. Initially, balancing being ethical or true to one's own needs while simultaneously being loyal in meeting expectations and obligations to others, especially our spouse or romantic partner, can feel like walking a tightrope without a safety net, but over time you find that together you are weaving a sacred safety net for each other through the sacrifices you make to be reciprocally fully cooperative and fully assertive. The CAST approach teaches that there is a safety net in the form of collaboration with and commitment to your partner.

Let me tell another personal story about collaboration, trust, sacrifice, effort, needs, and loyalty. As relative newlyweds in graduate school, my wife asked for my cooperation on an important task she needed. She was preparing for a craft she was in charge of doing with the women of our church at an activity planned for that upcoming weekend. As part of the craft she needed twenty wooden hearts about the size of a cantaloupe cut out of 1" by 8" pine boards she had purchased. She requested that I go outside to our detached garage and cut out the wooden hearts with a jigsaw. Now mind you, unlike her father who was the ultimate handyman, I wasn't very good with tools. I thought my time would be better served studying or getting a head start on a paper I had to eventually write for school, but she was insistent that I do this task for her.

So, I was walking out to the garage murmuring and grumbling about it when this spiritual epiphany of thought about collaboration hit me. The thought was this: "She has the right to ask this of you. That's what husbands do." It was followed up with a corollary thought about commitment: "You knew what she was like when you married her, and you signed up for it anyway." I came to the crystal-clear realization that day that my wife had the right to be highly assertive and ask for my full cooperation (basically collaboration). I also learned the power of commitment to vows. So, I did my best to cut out those wooden hearts, but the real prize was that my heart was softened. Eventually, I came to realize that this collaboration expectation in marriage worked in the other direction. I had the right to also be highly assertive and expect her full cooperation. Over the years, as we have collaborated through the highs and lows of life, there has been a sweetness that has come into our marriage because of our ability to rely on one another for collaboration. We often had to make some sacrifices for each other, and we often had to both sacrifice things for our children and the good of the whole family system. Those sacrifices became sacred threads of trust and commitment in the safety net of our lives together. These predictable patterns of collaboration and commitment have forged a deep, abiding trust between each other. I can depend on her for anything, and she can do the same for me. We have become each other's safety net through life. Forging your own history of predictable patterns of collaboration and commitment is how you and your partner can develop trust and begin your ascent along the TRAIL to Love.

Think back to a time when you sacrificed, cooperated, or out yourself out there and really collaborated with your partner on something they needed? How did you feel when it was all done? Did you grumble a lot in the beginning, but in the end were glad you helped? Or was there lingering resentment?

Partner 1:
_____
_____
_____

Partner 2:
_____
_____
_____

Trust Comes from Positive Interactions and Not Absorbing Nasty Interactions Between Each Other

It all begins with small interactions. Each of you can "choose the right" cycle in your relationship day by day. Will you choose to act from a positive position of collaboration and choose the kind of trust that reduces resentment (a positive CTR cycle)? Or, will you cling to your resentment, be distrustful, and withhold your cooperation choosing instead a different conflict resolution style such as compromising, competing, accommodating, or avoiding that leads to a neutral or negative CTR cycle?

Dr. Ivan Boszormenyi-Nagy said that trust arises from the "regularity and predictability of certain repetitious events in families" including multiple generations of families.[16] What kind of regular, predictable, and repetitious family events do you want to have in your relationship based on the Nice-Nice, Neutral-Neutral, or Nasty-Nasty interactions that Dr. Gottman describes? In truth, relationships experience all of the above throughout the course of years, but Dr. Gottman further helps us understand that *the really detrimental pattern that erodes trust is the Nasty-Nasty interactions.*

Dr. Gottman[17] indicates that while all couples will engage in a Nasty-Nasty interaction from time to time, happy couples tend to be what he calls "non-absorbing." These happy couples maintain their positive perspective on one another because they tend to have much difficulty getting into a Nasty-Nasty interaction, and when they do fall into the undesirable interaction, they are quick to get out of it. Essentially, happy couples do not absorb the nasty negativity cycle into their relationship easily because they don't get into the Nasty-Nasty cycle easily, but when they do get into such a cycle, they find an easy way out of the trapping nastiness. In contrast unhappy couples are often in an absorbing state of negativity because they easily fall into Nasty-Nasty interactions and have great difficulty getting out of them. The time and energy they spend in such Nasty-Nasty interactions seems to erode their trust like acid eroding enamel. So, avoiding Nasty-Nasty interactions as much as possible, and getting out of them as quickly as you can if you find yourself in one is the key lesson here.

What are you best ways of quickly getting out of a "Nasty-Nasty" interaction with your partner? When have you had success either avoiding a Nasty-Nasty interaction or getting out of them quickly? Write down your experiences.

PARTNER 1:
_____
_____
_____

PARTNER 2:
_____
_____
_____

BUILDING TRUST AFTER BETRAYAL – *Twelve Crucial Steps of Rebuilding Trust*[18*]

Oftentimes, marriages and other forms of relational partnering have had deep wounds and serious betrayals of trust in their history.

It is not uncommon for therapists to have couples come to our offices with stories of addictions, infidelities, and other behaviors where trust has been demolished by significant betrayals. While trust may be difficult to restore, with time and great effort even these deep violations can be assuaged and trust rebuilt or renewed. Healing and trusting again is possible. Discontinuing those behaviors that violate trust is the key first step. It may be necessary for the addict (in cases of addiction) to enter a treatment program before couples therapy can be fully effective. Affairs need to end and a determination to address problems that may have existed in the relationship even prior to the affair needs to be secured. But change is possible, and restoring trust is an essential priority. In a subsequent chapter we will deal with healing the deep attachment wounds that come from such betrayals, but for now, I'd like to focus on the trust elements of repairing the relationship.

After discontinuing the betraying behavior, there are twelve crucial steps to rebuilding trust:[19]

1. Turning Toward One Another
2. Clear Admission of Faults and Secrets (Therapist-Guided Full Disclosure)
3. Expression of Genuine Remorse – The Apology[20]

- Expressing Regret – "I'm sorry"
- Accepting Responsibility – "I was wrong"
- Making Restitution – "What can I do to make it right?"
- Genuinely Repenting – "I'll try not to do that again"
- Requesting Forgiveness – "Will you please forgive me?"

4. Transparency with Verification
5. Process and Understand the History and Factors of the Betrayal
6. Process Emotional Wounds from Betrayal
7. Increase Reciprocal Cooperation (Jumpstart a CTR+ Cycle)

. . .

8. Commit to Mutually Meeting Each Other's Needs through Collaboration.

9. Establish a High Cost for Subsequent Betrayals (Bottom Lines)

10. Emotional Attunement is Established or Enhanced

11. Forgiveness and Enhancing Capacity to Mentally and Emotionally Let Go

12. Consistently Repair and Strengthen the Collaborative Story of "Us"

THE KEY BEGINNING of rebuilding trust is Gottman's principle of "turning toward each other" rather than away from each other. Turning toward one another is an openness (which eventually leads to the next step on the TRAIL to Love – Regard) to connect with each other through bids for affection, attention, and attunement. It takes increasing our vulnerability and being willing to try again. Each partner needs to "tune in" to the others emotions, needs, hurts, and desires. We need to look to one another, rather than outside sources for comfort and solace.

Next, the offending partner needs to fully admit and disclose the elements of their betrayal. This unburdening of secrets is as important to the offending partner as it is the non-offending partner. Any secret-keeping will lead the offending partner to maintain shame, which generally leads them back to the betraying behavior or addiction cycle. The offended partner has a right to know what he or she is dealing with in order to determine if they will eventually be able to forgive. This full disclosure process usually goes very badly if done without the aid of a therapist to guide the couple through the disclosure process. It is highly recommended that the therapist take the time to facilitate a healthy disclosure process for all concerned.

Expressing genuine remorse and properly apologizing is something both Dr. Gottman and Drs. Chapman and Thomas highly recommend. Of particular note for proper apologizing is Chapman and Thomas' book *The Five Languages of Apology*. It is important that apologies don't make excuses, turn the offending partner into a victim, or otherwise manipulate the person being apologized to. Apologies have the five critical elements of expressing regret, accepting responsibility, making restitution, genuinely repenting or forsaking the betraying behaviors, and requesting forgiveness.[21]

The betraying spouse also has to become transparent – an open book – subject to verification. As mentioned previously, transparency facilitates trust because it is the evidence that the person is *being trustworthy*. This evidence verification process builds confidence as time goes on without any further betrayals. Being transparent and forthright with each other when you have nothing to hide is an advantage trusting relationships can build on. I once worked with a sexual addiction addict whose wife demanded that he give her all the passwords to his phone, email accounts, and social media. He protested, "What about my privacy?" This lasted for weeks as they debated back and forth and the wife was very close to separating from him. Finally, I leveled with him, "You know how this will play out with your wife and daughters (he had only daughters), don't you? They will side with your wife. You can have your privacy or your family, but you can't have both." He wisely chose to relinquish the passwords and became completely transparent. In the end, he and his wife were able to reconcile, work on rebuilding trust in their relationship in therapy, and he overcame his addiction issues. Their family was spared the devastation of continuing down his addictive path because he was willing to be transparent.

The couple also has to be willing to talk and process the history of the betrayal patterns and the causal factors (ideally with the help of a therapist) so they can understand what happened to them and how to avoid it in the future. By understanding what happened, why it happened, and how to prevent it from happening again, the couple can gain confidence that things will be different in their relationship as they move forward. Remember that exploring the causal factors does not mean making excuses for the betraying behavior or condoning it. Rather, it is an attempt to learn what happened and how to be on guard against its future occurrence.

Processing the emotional wounds from the betrayal is often the longest and most painful step of rebuilding trust. While more will be described in a subsequent chapter about how to build a better attachment relationship to heal deep, serious relational wounds, it is important to note that processing the hurt wounds so that the offended partner can either heal or ward off trauma is necessary and often takes more time that the offending partner would like. It is very common that when the offended partner processes their emotional wounds that the offending partner goes into deep shame mode. The offending partner needs to be able to hear and process their partners hurt wounds without defensiveness or shaming themselves. While guilt focuses on behavior and holds people accountable, guilt's counterfeit cousin of shame focuses on identity and drives people to self-pity or self-loathing – not change or correction of behavior.

Gottman suggests that increasing reciprocal cooperation is another important factor in rebuilding trust. I would point out that by focusing on jumpstarting a positive Collaboration-Trust-Resentment (CTR+) cycle, the couples will inherently increase reciprocal cooperation along with other activating forces (increasing assertiveness and lowering resentment) that will foster trust.

Specifically focusing on mutually meeting one another's needs through collaboration efforts further builds trust. Particularly, as the couple increases their investment and mutual dependency on one another, their "pro-relationship" thoughts will blossom.[22] At this point in the process of reforming trust, mutual collaboration in meeting one another's needs builds more emotional connection that will spur us to the next step in the TRAIL of Love (Regard) in short order.

At this mid-phase of rebuilding trust after betrayal, Gottman emphasizes the importance of clear norms or rules that establish "high costs"[23] for subsequent betrayals. This does not necessarily mean placing "ultimatums" on one's spouse or partner, but there does need to be a clear understanding of the ramifications that will accompany subsequent betrayals. In the LifeStar program for sexual addiction treatment, we encourage people to establish bottom lines for themselves, personally, and for their relationship. This is an area where a spouse or partner should share their bottom lines about what they will and will not tolerate in themselves and in their relationship.

Emotional attunement – how responsive and attentive we are to our partner's feelings and expressions – helps soothe or heal broken trust at this point. Couples need to learn how to talk intimately and attentively with one another. They must practice reading cues and striving to establish or enhance high emotional attunement with each other.

The last two steps center around forgiveness and maintaining relational strength. Forgiveness can be difficult after serious betrayals, yet there are significant advantages to forgiving your partner. Volumes of books have been written about the benefits of forgiveness, specifically in terms of the health benefits of the forgiving and letting go of grudges, but letting go can be hard to do. During the early 1920's a young Jewish woman, Bluma Zeigarnik, noticed how waiters could remember people's orders with great detail, but later when the customers were gone, she interviewed the waiters and they could not recall the information.[24] What Gottman calls the "Zeigarnik effect" essentially means we tend to hold onto or recall things that we have not fully processed or are not complete. Once we have finished completing what we need the information for, we often no longer retain the information. You may have noticed that when you cram for a test you can recall much of the information but once the exam is over you retain very little of what you studied – that's because your mind has recognized that you are finished needing that information and it gets wiped clean. Before the test, the Zeigarnik effect is working causing you to retain the information, but after the test the

Zeigarnick effect releases the information. If you are having a hard time forgiving your partner's offence and letting go of the betrayal mentally or emotionally, you may be experiencing the Zeigarnik effect (or possibly some level of trauma). The key to letting go of the painfulness of the betrayal may lie in completely processing the thoughts and feelings with your spouse and therapist until your brain and heart realize you do not need that information anymore. You may come to realize that dwelling on the thoughts, memories, and feelings about the betrayal is no longer protecting you (which was its original purpose) but is now instead hurting you needlessly or at least holding you back from growth and progress in your life. This may be how you will know you are ready to forgive, drop your resentments, stop ruminating on the hurtful events, and let it go mentally and emotionally.

Recognize that even after you have forgiven and let go of the be betrayals in your relationship, there will always be new moments of hurt, disconnect, and fallibility. We are all human and make mistakes. You will need to use repair attempts repeatedly and frequently in your relationship. But rather than feeling like you are "going back to square one" every time there is a mishap in the relationship, strive to normalize the process of trial and error in every relationship and use repair attempts to strengthen your relationship. Particularly, focus on what I sometimes call "the Story of Us" – your love story which also now has a chapter on how you overcame significant betrayals, obstacles, and challenges and learned to collaborate with one another to build a united couple identity. This couple identity will be a crucial resource as you continue along the TRAIL of Love.

Which of the 12 Crucial Steps to Rebuilding Trust do you feel you each need to work on? Where do you two tend to get stuck?

Partner 1:
_____
_____
_____

Partner 2:

_____
_____
_____

HOMEWORK – **Chapter 1: Trust Sharing**

At a time of your choosing, plan to share something you haven't been fully transparent around. For starters, consider allowing your partner to go through your phone asking questions as they peruse it. For the person going through the device, they should not attack or blame. For the person opening up and being transparent, try to respond without being defensive.

Maybe you would prefer to share a story or experience you never told your partner about before or feel the need to apologize for. Perhaps this story was "too embarrassing" or maybe you felt justified in keeping it a secret. If your fear the experience might potentially be too "volatile" consider asking your therapist to help you prepare what to say, or you may choose to have the experience of sharing occur during a therapy session where the counselor can guide and monitor the interaction.

RECOMMENDED **Readings**

- John M. Gottman (2011). *The Science of Trust: Emotional Attunement for Couples.* New York, NY: W.W. Norton & Co.
- Gary Chapman and Jennifer Thomas (2006). *The Five Languages of Apology: How to Experience Healing in All Your Relationships.* Chicago, IL: Northfield Publishing.

CHAPTER TWO - REGARD

Regard is a funny word. It has multiple, related definitions. Regard can mean the following possible definitions: "to have a protective interest" in or care for, a "feeling of respect or affection," a "friendly greeting with much feeling," or to hold someone or something as having "great worth or estimation."[1] In CAST the term "regard" is used to include a whole lot of interrelated things, as well. *Primarily, regard is used to convey a tenderness of affection, a personal fondness or liking for your partner, an admiration of your partner's qualities, a preoccupation with the characteristics of your partner, a quality of fun and playfulness, and an openness that stems from feelings of safety and protection that enables you to socially engage and be emotionally attuned with your partner.* Regard involves a deeper, more vulnerable level of connection and affection than trust, but not quite as deep as the subsequent steps of attachment, intimacy, and love that remain further down the TRAIL of Love. I like to say that when it comes to the stage of regard, "things get personal."

You might trust your business partner, a neighbor, or a doctor, but if you were to be honest with yourself, that's probably because you know if they did something wrong like a business partner breaching a contract, a neighbor wrecking your fence, or a doctor engaging in malpractice you could sue for redress and enforce the terms of your relationship expectations as far as they go. But when you are talking about trusting a spouse or romantic partner, it takes on a whole new level of meaning and vulnerability. When things get really personal like that, you are not only trusting them, you feel affection, connection, safety, fondness, admiration, enjoyment, and respect – in other words, you feel *regard* for them.

If you remember the five-tiered wedding cake in the introduction, you might say that if you were climbing up the tiers of the cake that on the second level you are standing on regard *and* trust because trust is underneath regard and supports it. You need trust to successfully feel regard for your partner. With regard, we use what we gained at the trust level and bring it to bear with regard. Just as you had to be vulnerable to a degree to trust your partner at the first stage of the TRAIL to Love, with the second stage (Regard) you will have to increase your vulnerability.

Regard usually begins by reading social and emotional cues from your partner and assessing your safety in the interaction. The safety and emotional attunement you acquire from developing trust in the first stage of the TRAIL to Love is what underlies and empowers the development of the second stage – Regard. Without the safety and emotional attunement of trust, you cannot become increasingly vulnerable to develop regard. If you perceive a threat may be lurking, you are likely to do one of two things: fight or flee.

The fight or flight response has been studied by many researchers, but one particular researcher has much to offer in this matter. Dr. Stephen Porges, a "Distinguished University Scientist" at the Kinsey Institute at Indiana University Bloomington and Professor of Psychiatry at the University of North Carolina-Chapel Hill, is the author of the book *The Polyvagal Theory: Neurophysiological Foundations of Emotions, Attachment, Communication, and Self-Regulation.*[2] While the book is fairly complex with biological, medical, and physiological terminology, the basic premise is that humans respond to levels of threat based on how our nervous systems respond to perceived threats. When we feel safe and calm, we are socially open and engaging. We seek connection, can be compassionate, are curious, and feel grounded or settled. That is because we are operating the Ventral Vagal Complex (VVC) of our parasympathetic nervous system. When we perceive some level of threat or danger, we switch to the sympathetic nervous system and our state of arousal increases. Dr. Porges measured "heart rate variability" to determine physiological responses to threat. While in the sympathetic nervous system, our "fight or flight" response kicks in. On the fight side we may experience frustration, irritation, anger, and rage as our arousal levels increase. On the flight side we may experience worry or concern, anxiety, fear, or panic in successive order. When the danger or threat is perceived as severe or life threatening, we once again enter the parasympathetic nervous system but this time we are utilizing the Dorsal Vagal Complex (DVC) rather than the Ventral Vagal Complex (VVC) (hence the term "polyvagal" because multiple vagal complexes are utilized in response to threats). In this extremely high level of threat, our response is to "freeze" rather than fight or flee. We will experience feelings of helplessness, depression, numbness or even dissociation, as well as shame, hopelessness, and feeling trapped. The following figure illustrates the key responses to threat according to the polyvagal theory.

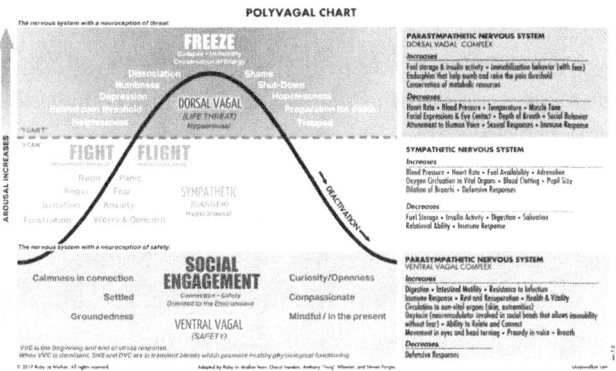

Figure 1 - Summary of Polyvagal Theory

Used by permission courtesy of Ruby Jo Walker, LCSW

YOU MAY NOT HAVE CONSCIOUSLY REALIZED ALL that was going on inside your nervous systems at a time when you and your partner were arguing, but your nervous systems were picking up on cues and responding to the level of threat accordingly. Learning to remain calm, reduce physiological arousal or "flooding,"[3] and viewing your partner as your collaborative teammate rather than your enemy is important to your ability to develop regard for him or her. You need to feel safe in order to be curious and get to know or understand your partner better and have feelings of fondness and admiration for them. "Staying in the green" area (the lower state of calmness that lends to social engagement) of the polyvagal chart is crucial for building a healthier relationship and moving forward on the TRAIL to Love. Seeing your partner as a collaborative teammate, instead of an enemy or threat, will help you feel regard and eventually attach to them.

Your previous work to develop trust in your partner also helps you "stay in the green" portion of the polyvagal chart. That is how trust leads to the second stage of regard. Now that you are more socially open, engaged, and calm, you can begin to develop a more personal relationship by having more fun and playfulness in your relationship, getting to know your partner better, feeling more fondness and admiration for him or her, and having more affection as you build regard. *I believe regard is a concept with those dimensions of social engagement, playfulness, love maps, fondness and admiration, and affection with emotional attunement as the underlying force driving those dimensions.* The perception of safety that stems from trust allows emotional attunement to begin its work as you socially engage one another, have fun or enjoyable interactions, know each other better by building "love maps," increase your fondness and admiration, and feel greater affection for one another. Each of these critical dimensions of regard requires emotional attunement to be an operative, driving force in your marriage.

THE TRAIL TO LOVE

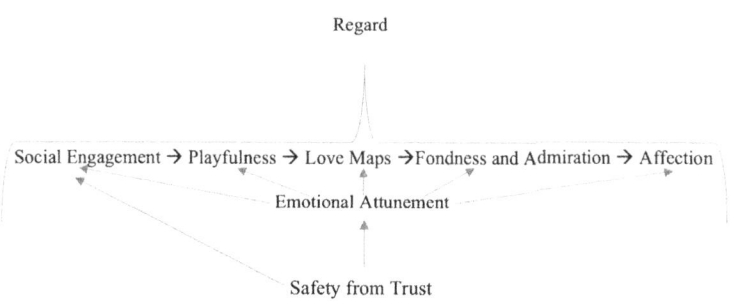

Figure 2 Regard with Sub-Dimensions

EMOTIONAL ATTUNEMENT

As you developed trust in the previous stage, you activated two powerful elements that are critical to developing regard. You became more emotionally attuned to each other and you became more socially open and engaged with one another. Emotional attunement is so essential to building a better relationship. Emotional attunement is essentially being aware of and responding appropriately to each other's emotions. Dr. Gottman details six dimensions to emotional attunement and uses the acronym ATTUNE to describe these dimensions:

"<u>A</u>wareness of the emotion
<u>T</u>urning toward the emotions
<u>T</u>olerance of the emotional experience
<u>U</u>nderstanding the emotion
<u>N</u>ondefensive Listening to the emotion
<u>E</u>mpathy toward the emotion"[4]

EMOTIONAL ATTUNEMENT ALLOWS you and your spouse or partner to learn how to relate to one another emotionally. Perhaps your partner shares that they are going through something difficult in their lives (say for example, a work conflict with a colleague or a dispute with an extended relative) and they want to express their feelings to you. By following the six dimensions of attunement you would start by being aware of their feelings and emotions, turn toward the emotions (engage your partner) and be open to hearing about them, tolerate the emotional experience (meaning sit with the feelings without running away from or deflecting emotions that may be uncomfortable), understand what your partner is feeling, listen non-defensively (meaning don't try to protect or defend yourself), and show empathy with the emotions by expressions that demonstrate that you relate to what they are feeling (without taking the conversation over and making it about yourself).

PRACTICE BREAK – Emotional Attunement

The six-step process of attuning may be easier to practice when your partner shares feelings about something that doesn't relate directly to you or if you share feelings about something that doesn't directly relate to them. Start by practicing sharing your feelings with one another and seeking to be emotionally attuned with each other by picking something you have important feelings about that is not directly related to the two of you or your relationship. Be certain to share emotions or feelings (sadness, anger, loneliness, and so forth), not just share what happened in the experience. For example, when practicing sharing feelings about a co-worker, relative, situation, or scenario external to your marriage or romantic partnership, don't just say what happened – say how you *felt* about what happened. After each of you take turns sharing feelings with the other practicing the six-steps of emotional attunement, write down what it was like for you at each step:

Partner 1:
Awareness of the emotion
_____

Turning toward the emotions
_____

Tolerance of the emotional experience
_____

Understanding the emotion
_____

Nondefensive Listening to the emotion
_____

Empathy toward the emotion
_____

PARTNER 2:

Awareness of the emotion
_____

Turning toward the emotions
_____

Tolerance of the emotional experience
_____

Understanding the emotion
_____

Nondefensive Listening to the emotion
_____

Empathy toward the emotion
_____

Emotional attunement is really the driving force for the other dimensions of regard. That is why it is so important to practice and become good at emotional attunement. Once you are good at being emotionally attuned with your partner on things not directly related to just the two of you, it may be time to practice being emotionally attuned to one another about things that are directly focused on your relationship. It would be a good idea to ask you therapist to spend a session or two helping you practice honing your emotional attunement skills. Think of your therapist as an emotions coach to help train you to be emotionally attuned with one another and facilitate your emotional regulation. Be sure to take the time to master and refine this skill of emotional attunement. It is critical for your success in developing the remainder of the principles of regard that you will need.

Social Engagement and *Openness*

The safety you developed in the trust stage of the TRAIL to Love directly impacts your ability to be socially open and engaged with your partner. But because the safety of trust also allows you to become more emotionally attuned with one another (and emotional attunement further reduces threat and creates more openness and engagement as outlined in Porges' polyvagal theory), the safety of trust also has an indirect relationship to your social openness and engagement through emotional attunement. That's why in Figure 10 earlier in this chapter there are two arrows pointing towards the development of social engagement. Social engagement is important because it starts the ball rolling on the remaining dimensions under regard. It involves "staying in the green" or lowest portion of the Polyvagal Chart (Figure 1). Interestingly, staying calm, settled, grounded, curious, open, compassionate, and mindful in the moment as outlined by the green section of the Polyvagal Chart not only helps you have a healthier relationship, it helps you remain physically healthy, as well. As you decrease defensiveness and are socially engaged, you benefit by things like resistance to infection, better digestion, are more restful, and breathe better which leads to your ability to relate, connect, and socially bond. So "staying in the green" and being socially open and engaging is a powerful element of building regard.

Many people find mindfulness practices helpful in remaining calm and open. Taking a few minutes each day to stop, breathe calmly and deeply from your diaphragm, and then be mindful in the moment of your feelings is powerful. You can add a self-compassion dimension by thinking about how what you may be going through links you with the common human experiences of others and to give yourself positive thoughts and words of encouragement to help you face your challenges. Other people find spiritual or religious practices such as prayer, scripture study, meditation, or experiences in nature (such as a walk in the woods or a park) to help them "stay in the green" and be calm, grounded, settles, and open. The key is to find things that work for you and your partner to have reduced perceptions of threat and increased calmness, safety, and openness so that you can engage with one another as your best selves.

Fun, Playfulness, and Enjoyment

Think back to your first dating experiences. For most people, one of the conditions of getting a second or subsequent date is how much fun you had on a prior date. Fun, playfulness, and mutual enjoyment play a critical role at the beginning of romantic relationships. But somewhere along the way, we sometimes forget to continue having fun. When the mundane pressures of life creep in (bills, rent or mortgage, kids' schedules, and so forth), we sometimes let fun and playfulness in the couple's relationship take a back seat to these more pressing demands. Quality marriages and other forms of couple relationships that are highly successful and satisfying place a premium on maintaining fun, playfulness, and mutual enjoyment of each other. We tend not to have a high personal regard with people we find boring, grumpy, and lacking fun. Playfulness is an essential quality to building regard. The openness and willingness to connect we find from social engagement lends the opportunity to move forward into playfulness.

Sometimes I hear a partner complain that the other person in their relationship lacks spontaneity. I take some time to explore what they have in mind by "spontaneity." More often than not, they come to the conclusion that they aren't really looking for the impulsiveness and randomness that goes along with spontaneity. What they are really searching for is the playfulness they once had in their relationship that has been dimmed by the pressures of life and "boring" monotony of their routine. I counsel that while no one can plan to be spontaneous (because planning is antithetical to spontaneity), people can plan to be playful. Focusing plans and efforts on playfulness usually revives the sense of regard they are seeking.

WHAT ARE some things you and your partner did when you first started dating or early on in the relationship that were fun and enjoyable? Which of those activities and experiences would you like to bring back and do more of in your relationship now?

Partner 1:
_____
_____
_____

Partner 2:
_____
_____
_____

KNOWING Each Other Better through Love Maps

The next two dimensions of regard derive directly from Dr. Gottman's book *Seven Principles for Making Marriage Work* – enhancing your love maps and nurturing your fondness and admiration for your partner.[5] Love maps are essentially the cognitive space you make in your brain to know and remember things that are important about and to your partner. At the beginning stage of most relationships, couples invest considerable time and effort to "get to know" each other. But for some reason, we tend to stop doing that as much as the relationship progresses. Perhaps we think we already know enough about our partner and what they think and feel about a situation. Ironically, research shows that the longer we are in a relationship with someone, the *less* likely we can accurately predict their thoughts, feelings, and opinions about matters of preference.[6] Why? Mostly, because we have stopped listening to them, think we know them too well, and forget that people grow and change over time. That is why we have to be continually working and updating our love maps of our partners on an ongoing basis. We need to ask about things we know are happening in their lives. In the morning of each day, we should learn one or two things that they anticipate happening that day and then call and check in to see how those things went. Maybe it is as simple as learning and then calling or texting about how a doctor's appointment or a lunch meeting with the boss went, or simply asking how their day is going. We can also seek deeper levels of knowledge such as their feelings about an aging family member nearing convalescence or death, their frustrations with a long-term project or concern that there are no easy answers for, or what they hope to accomplish over a specified time period in their professional or personal endeavors. The point of love maps is to truly *know* your partner by continually listening to and checking in with your partner. This is essential for your regard or personal affection to grow.

Try to discover one new thing about your spouse or partner (or something about them that has changed since you started dating) this week that you didn't know about them before and write it down here:

PARTNER 1:

_____

_____

. . .

PARTNER 2:

_____
_____

FONDNESS AND ADMIRATION

The correlate or subsequent step to love maps in Gottman's model is nurturing your "fondness and admiration" system[7] in your relationship. When you think back on the history of your relationship, what good times come to mind? What memories do you have when you really admired or felt fond of your partner? Every long-term relationship has good and bad times during the ups and downs of life. Focusing on the good times is important in reminding yourself why you fell in love with your partner in the first place.

Take a moment and list five things that you admire about your partner – things that remind you why you are fond of them:

Partner 1:

1. _____
2. _____
3. _____
4. _____
5. _____

PARTNER 2:

1. _____
2. _____
3. _____
4. _____
5. _____

Engaging in the practice of looking for positives in your partner, praising them where possible, and expressing gratitude can have significant benefits. Establishing a system of keeping your fondness, admiration, and positivity about your partner flourishing is a powerful antidote to what Gottman calls the "Four Horsemen of the Apocalypse" – criticism, contempt, defensiveness, and stonewalling.[8] Criticism is any type of personal, negative attack toward a partner. While we sometimes have to bring up complaints in our relationships in order to improve things, there's a difference between a criticism and a complaint. Complaints focus on behavior that needs to be changed without attacking the person. Criticism is when we attack the person themselves – which should be avoided at all costs in a marriage. We should also ensure that we keep our positive praise to negative complaint ratio very much in the positive direction – at least five positives should be expressed for every one negative comment or complaint (and actually more than five positives to every negative is even better when possible). If criticism goes unchecked for too long, the criticizing partner and the criticized counterpart may both end up feeling contempt for one another – the opposite of regard. Contempt for our partner sours the outlook and perceptions we have of nearly everything our partner does. If your spouse is asking you to give them the "benefit of the doubt" frequently in your relationship, there may be a contempt problem in your relationship. Contempt distorts our perceptions of the reality into *mis*perceptions. Our attributions or story we tell ourselves about our partners actions and motivations more often than not become *mis*attributions. It can be compared to "seeing through a glass darkly," like putting on sunglasses while driving on an already dark night – and contempt is probably just as dangerous for your relationship. Contempt leads to defensiveness. Defensiveness is the opposite of collaboration – it escalates conflict rather than resolving it. It comes in many forms – blaming, minimizing, rationalizing, and so much more. Defensiveness leads us back into the realm of selfishness and competitiveness. The final horseman is stonewalling. When the criticism, contempt, and defensiveness reach their crescendo, one or both partners begin to tune out, give up, or claim the "right to remain silent." Essentially, they are signaling they are willing to cooperate with their partner about as much as a stone wall is willing to budge. Like politicians who vote "present" rather than be involved in a yea or nay vote, the partner's silent resistance is saying upfront that they are still here physically but they have mentally and emotionally checked out. This is the avoiding style of conflict with a defiant, resentful, and "Nasty-Nasty" attitude.

Fondness and admiration reverse the four horsemen – breaking the walls and barriers between the two battle weary foes. Often a leading spouse has to take the leap of faith, increase their collaboration efforts and trust, and attempt a significant repair to convert the negative cycle that the four horsemen cause. Expressing fondness, admiration, and gratitude can be an effective repair in and of itself, at times and bolster a CTR conversion towards the positive.

I recall an occasion where my wife and I were not on the same page and there was some tension in our marriage. We had just moved to Fresno and it was my first semester teaching at Fresno State. In addition to teaching my classes, I was eager to begin writing several scholarly journal articles that were necessary to achieve tenure. My wife's focus was more on unpacking our things into the house we just moved into, wrangling the then-five young kids we had into some semblance of order, and making our house into a home for our family. Each had asserted our needs, but I confess my cooperation was less than the ideal high she deserved. I justified my lack of cooperation with the demands of the new job, but I couldn't help feeling I was letting some defensiveness I didn't really want creep into the marriage. One Monday evening after a late-night class ended, I sat at my office desk at work trying to pack up and go home for the day. I gave myself the luxury of spending an extra few minutes reviewing old computer files of half-written articles that maybe I could complete quickly and get sent off soon. I found one on the concept of gratitude in marriage that I thought might have some promise of publishing merit. I thought to myself, "I should finish writing this." My next thought was, "I should live this." I decided to try an experiment that week and express gratitude to my wife at least once a day if not more. Instead of telling her what I was doing upfront (I usually tell her my half-baked ideas upfront), I decided I would just do the experiment of expressing gratitude daily without letting her in on what I was doing and see how things went. The change was remarkable! Less than a week later the two of us were driving somewhere and I asked, 'Have you noticed anything different this week?" She teasingly retorted, "Yeah, I like you better." We laughed and I explained my experiment in expressing daily gratitude. I was astounded at how quickly repeated, frequent expressions of gratitude could turn our marriage relationship around. The gratitude reminded both of us of what we admired in one another – it activated our fondness and admiration system. If you focus on the positive qualities you see in your partner and express your gratitude, fondness, and admiration to them, it will likely cause healthier relationship patterns in your companionship.

AFFECTION

Many married couples remember the affection they had with one another during their honeymoon with fondness. Some wish that feeling between them could last forever. A manual for married life published in 1875 has a chapter called "How to Establish a Perfect Affection," which gave this counsel to newlyweds about how to maintain that level of affection throughout the years of their marriage:

> "Yet why not make your honey-moon a honey-annum? Why cut it short in thirty days? Love is now your most important life *business*: then shape business to it, not it to business. That good old Biblical custom which excused every young husband from war; public service, &c, the first married year, requiring him to 'stay at home,' and 'comfort his wife,' should be modernized. After your mutual affections are once well started, they will grow on without special nurture.
>
> "THIS IS YOUR GREAT LIFE-LABOR. Think how great; and how infinitely important that it be commenced not about but *just* right; which requires time. No great work can be finished up hastily; and the

greater, the longer its incipiency. Neglect other things, but take time enough to make this thorough. Surrender yourselves wholly to it. Let it imbue and engross your whole beings."[9]

The gist of the counsel is to develop "mutual affections" carefully from the beginning, prioritize it over other concerns of life, and invest considerable time to building affectionate relationships. Building and maintaining affection in your relationship is a matter of priority and time, but it is also a matter of safety and emotional attunement which we have been working on in this chapter, as well as the prior chapter. Dr. Don Catherall, a Clinical Associate Professor at Northwestern University and author of the book *Emotional Safety*, writes about what he calls *affective resonance* – how we interactively respond to one another's emotions.[10] In some ways affective resonance can be contagious. Have you ever been in a perfectly fine mood, and then interacted with your partner or another person in a foul mood turning your mood upset and sour? That's affective resonance. It took several years of marriage for me to learn that just because my wife was mad at me didn't mean I needed to be mad back at her. I learned I could put up what Dr. Catherall calls an *empathic wall* – a boundary that moderates, limits, or allows some affective resonance through to me without permitting too much feeling that would overwhelm my emotions. Think of the empathic wall like a filter that allows some amount of emotion from your partner to pass through to you, but not so much that you are overwhelmed and can't process your own feelings. Some couples have an empathic wall that is too rigid and they are distant, cold, and unfeeling toward one another. Others have barely an empathic wall at all – they react and bounce off of each other's emotions with little to no control at all. Getting this boundary or empathic wall to not be too hard or too soft, but "just right" (kind of like from the story of Goldilocks and the Three Bears) is an important task – one we will review further in a subsequent chapter.

Ideally, the safety and emotional attunement you gained from the trust stage have enabled you to be socially open and engaged, as well as playful with your spouse or partner. You have gone on to develop your love maps as you got to know your partner more deeply, and have nurtured your fondness and admiration of your partner. The culmination of this previous work typically leads to positive affectionate feelings for your partner.

Expressing your affectionate feelings through physical connection is important. Typically, couples express their affections through touch, hand holding, hugging, kissing, and other tender gestures. Affectionate expressions such as these, as well as verbal affectionate gestures, are your way of communicating to your partner your positive feelings. These positive tokens of affection allow for the empathic wall to come down and your affective resonance to influence one another. This is why a hug or a kiss can be so consoling in a time of sorrow, or can highlight interest and playfulness when you are enjoying a good time with your partner.

Making expressions of affection a priority shows that you are being intentional about your relationship. It also shows you are willing to put other concerns aside and take the time to build affection with your partner. Dr. Gottman writes about the "Magic Six Hours"[11] happy couples spend each week to ensure a healthy marriage. In our daily goings and comings – our partings and reunions – we should express affection with a hug and a kiss, as well as learn one thing that is happening in our spouse's life that day before saying goodbye and then hug, kiss, and have a short conversation (about 20 minutes) to reconnect when we return home. If our partings take 2 minutes a day over a five-day work week and our reunions take about 20 minutes a day over the same work-week, we will spend about 1 hour and 50 minutes in our comings and goings. Dr. Gottman also suggests spending five minutes a day verbally expressing affection, admiration, and appreciation for seven days a week and showing another five minutes each day engaging in physical affection each week. That equals 1 hour and 10 minutes each week. Notice how much affection is being expressed in the 3 hours thus far. That's a lot of hugging, kissing, hand holding, caressing, and verbally affirming one another on a consistent, daily basis. His other three hours a week include a 2-hour weekly date (where hopefully there will be some verbal and physical affection) and a 1-hour "state of the union" meeting to touch base on how the relationship is going and if anything needs to be addressed. He counsels to start with a softened tone to avoid a "harsh start-up" (how we start a conversation sets the affective tone, so it is best to start softly and gently) and end each session asking what we can do for our partner to feel more loved in the coming week. Couples who follow this pattern will have frequent consistent affection in their relationship.

PRACTICE BREAK – The 8-Hour Expiration on an Affectionate Kiss

A game you can play as a couple to ensure affection is repeated and on-going is to decide to place an eight-hour expiration on your affectionate kisses. When a close friend of mine got married the bishop introduced this game to him and his bride. If you decide that a kiss only lasts 8 hours, then when you wake up each morning after sleeping for 8 hours, you'd better kiss your spouse. Then an hour or so later, since you'll probably be at work for about 8 hours, you'd better just kiss your spouse again. When you get home after work, that kiss is about to expire so you'd better hurry up and kiss. Then at night before going to bed, you should kiss so that you can get 8 hours of sleep. Then repeat the next day. If at any point you have to be apart for more than eight hours (such as business travel or if one of you has to stay later than expected for work) you may have to renew your kiss virtually through a text, phone call, or love notes left behind to get you through the time period. They may not be as good as a real physical kiss, but you are still sending affectionate expressions to your beloved. Start playing this game today and see what it can do to the level of affection in your relationship.

COUPLE IDENTITY FORMATION – *"The Story of Us"*

Once you and your partner have developed regard through the process described in this chapter, you will find that you start to think differently. As trust and regard ripen and deepen, you will start to feel more like a relational unit and think in terms of "we" instead of "me." It is if there are three elements in your relationship – you, your partner, and "us" – the relationship. Think about when you started to think of yourself as a couple and not just two individuals. When did your relationship begin to take on a life of its own?

As you formed this couple identity you started interacting with other couples. You probably became known by a common shared surname – the "Smith's" or the "Rodriguez's" or whatever your surname may be. Developmentally, you probably stopped engaging in some activities or behaviors that you did when single and started spending your leisure time more often than not as a couple. Perhaps, when you were single you went "clubbing" – going to dance clubs where single people mingle and meet. But now as a couple, that probably isn't something you should do – or at least not do without your partner present with you. Instead, if you really like dancing, you might take a dance class as a couple and then maybe go out to eat afterward on a double date with other couples you meet there. The point is that you start being seen as a coupled unit and that the world needs to see you as a couple and respect that boundary.

Your couple identity comes with a story or narrative. It includes the story of how you met and fell in love, but as your marriage or relationship matures over the years you most likely add to that story the ups and downs, the successes and the challenges you and your partner have endured. If children have come into your family, that role of parenting also adds to your marital or relationship story. Your couple identity grows and you start to get attached to one another. This "Story of Us" is important for the next stage along the TRAIL to Love. Attachment is inherently about a pair – whether it is a parent-child pair, a sibling pair, or a romantic partnership. Your understanding of your identity as a couple becomes important to better attach to one another and later deepen your intimacy and love with one another.

TAKE a few moments to jointly write your initial love story:

WHAT CHALLENGES or obstacles have you successfully overcome in your relationship over time?

WHEN DID you feel like your couple identity really began to form – when you felt like you moved from "me" to "we"?

WHAT ARE THE CORE VALUES, attributes, or characteristics of your couple identity?

_____
_____
_____
_____
_____
_____
_____

HOMEWORK – Chapter 2: The Detectives for Good Game

Each day for a week, each of you plan to engage in at least one (if not more – more is better) loving, thoughtful act of kindness or service for your partner. Don't tell them what it is – let him or her guess. Go throughout the day looking for what good thing your partner is doing for you. Pretend you're a detective and look for clues of the good thing or things your partner is doing for you. At the end of the day, try to guess what your partner did for you and let them guess what you did for them. Be sure to reward each other for those good deeds with kisses and other affectionate gestures.

RECOMMENDED Readings

- Randi Gunther (2011). *When Love Stumbles: How to Rediscover Love, Trust, and Fulfillment in Your Relationship.* Oakland, CA: New Harbinger Publications.
- Don R. Catherall (2007). *Emotional safety: Viewing couples through the lens of affect.* New York, NY: Routledge.
- Stephen W. Porges (2011). *The Polyvagal Theory: Neurophysiological Foundations of Emotions, Attachment, Communication, and Self-Regulation.* New York, NY: W.W.

Norton & Co. (This one is very complex and uses lots of medical terms).
- Gottman, J.M & Silver, N. (2015). The *Seven Principles for Making Marriage Work*. New York, NY: Three Rivers Press (especially try the exercises he recommends on pp. 74-86).

CHAPTER 3 - ATTACHMENT: APPLIED

The next step in the TRAIL to Love is Attachment. In chapter three we reviewed the basic principles of Attachment Theory, but in this chapter we will address how to *apply* attachment principles in your relationship. Trust and Regard are initial steps towards a healthy attachment relationship with your partner. The safety, emotional attunement, engagement, fun, loving knowledge of one another, fondness, and affection that occurs in the two prior stages comes to fruition in attachment. You now see your couple identity as a relational unit, and are prepared to collaborate to really connect and meet your attachment needs in deeper, vulnerable ways.

Attachment begins to happen when you "turn toward" one another in what Dr. Gottman calls "bids" for attention.[1] Reaching out to your partner and having them "be there" for you in response is the elemental interaction that begins attachment. Once the bids for attention are *consistently* met with the other partner "turning toward" and responding to their partner's needs, the attachment relationship strengthens.

Both John Gottman and Sue Johnson address attachment and put forth the idea that attachment in a couple's relationship essentially boils down one partner's answer to the other's question: "Are you there for me?" But Gottman and Johnson have slightly different ways of analyzing that question.

Dr. Gottman seems to see his concept of trust to be nearly synonymous with attachment, though there is room for some distinctions. For Gottman, the answer to the question "Are you there for me?" appears to center on two concepts discussed earlier: transparency and ethics (or what he calls "positive moral certainty"). If a person knows their partner or spouse is being honest and open in a completely transparent manner, and if they also are certain that their spouse or partner is an ethical, good person with good intentions toward them, then the conditions in such a trusting relationship are ripe for attachment.

For Dr. Sue Johnson, the creator of Emotionally Focused Therapy (EFT), the "are" in "are you there for me?" is a power-packed acronym. Her version on the question is better expressed, "A.R.E. you there for me?" where the A stands for accessibility, the R stands for responsiveness, and the E stands for engaged.[2] In other words, one partner needs to know that the other partner is accessible, available, reachable, and present. If their partner is accessible, the next question is, "Are they responsive to me?" Will their partner not only be accessible but will they emotionally respond to their needs by listening and not stonewalling or shutting them out? If their partner is responsive, the third answer they need to know is if their partner will engage with them. Will their partner stay close to them, value them, and bring their heart, mind, muscle, or whatever other faculties that are needed to help find a solution to their dilemma?

TAKE a moment and each of you reflect on the "bids for attention" you frequently send to one another. How accessible, responsive, and engaged do you feel your partner is with you concerning your bids for attention?

. . .

WRITE down about a time when your partner was accessible, responsive, and engaged with you?

Partner 1:
_____
_____
_____

Partner 2:
_____
_____
_____

NOW WRITE about a time when your partner was not accessible or responsive or engaged (or all three were not present).

Partner 1:
_____
_____
_____

Partner 2:
_____
_____
_____

Write about what was different about the time when your partner was accessible, responsive, and engaged (A.R.E.) with you and the time when they weren't. Particularly, focus on what *feelings* came to you when they were accessible, responsive, and engaged with you compared to the time when they weren't.

Partner 1:
_____
_____

Partner 2:
_____
_____

PAYING attention to your feelings is especially important during the attachment stage (and subsequent stages) of the TRAIL to Love. As we strive to be more experiential and have you two *experience relating* differently to each other (as opposed to *talking* about how you relate to each other), your feelings become a priority. In fact, Dr. Sue Jonson's model Emotionally Focused Therapy states precisely your task in this stage of the TRAIL to Love – that you focus on your emotions and the emotions of your partner. Attachment is where emotional attunement becomes an advanced course of study and application. You have to become what I call **emotionally savvy** – meaning you become skilled, shrewd, and knowledgeable at a practical level about your own emotions and the emotions of your partner and what to do to enhance emotional connection in your relationship. Some have called this idea "emotional intelligence"[3] but I prefer the term emotionally savvy because it's not just about *knowing* or being intelligent about emotions that counts; it's about taking it to the next step where, after knowing your (and your partner's) emotions, you know what to *do* about those feelings. This can be hard to do. Some cultures don't value to expression of such deep, vulnerable feelings or have norms based on gender that could hinder such expressions. Or, you may have religious or ethnic factors that prescribe roles in family relationships. Yet, despite such variances stemming from diverse backgrounds, each culture still has unique ways that spouses and partners can develop strong and emotionally fulfilling marriages and romantic relationships. The methods of what to do may be different from one culture to another, but the fundamental objective of having an emotionally connected and fulfilling relationship remains the same. Work with your CAST trained therapist with such issues. They are trained to be sensitive to issues of culture, gender, religion, and other pertinent factors that may be an obstacle for such vulnerable, emotionally savvy expressions. They will help you discover together what the next steps are to move from

THE TRAIL TO LOVE

emotional intelligence to being emotionally savvy in your unique relationship.

Learning about how our behaviors – or tendencies in our actions (because no one is 100 percent consistent in their behaviors all the time) – affects our emotions and attachment needs at deep levels can be confusing at times, particularly when the stories, perceptions, and attributions about why our partner does what they do might be slightly biased or mysterious. On top of that there are patterns of interactive, systemic cycles going on between our partners and ourselves that overlay the whole matter. At times trying to understand the feelings and motivations of our partners and ourselves for why we do what we tend to do and feel what we feel can seem unfathomable. But fortunately, Emotionally Focused Therapy, has a model to explain what is going on. I have adapted Dr. Scott Woolley's EFT couples cycle diagram[4] to include elements of the CAST model in the following figure:

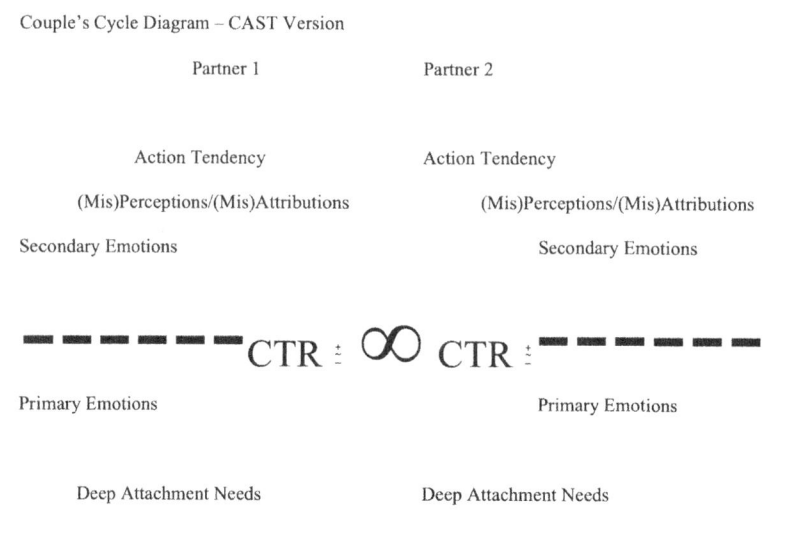

Figure 3. CAST Version of the Couple's Cycle

AS YOU AND your partner use trust and regard to develop a secure, connected attachment relationship, you will need to understand how

43

the cycle between the two of you affects you at the behavioral, cognitive, emotional, and deep attachment need levels.

If one partner makes a bid for attention or a bid for collaboration, how does the other partner respond? That may depend on several things including your history, moods, preoccupation with other matters, impending work demands, and probably several other things. The list could go on and on. But we are going to focus on the Collaboration-Trust-Resentment (CTR) cycle we reviewed in chapter four of this workbook. If you have a CTR+ (Nice-Nice interaction) or maybe even a CTR~ (Neutral-Neutral) interaction or some combination of intrapersonal and interpersonal Nice and Neutral interactions, things will probably be okay in your relationship interaction at the moment. These positive or neutral CTR cycles will likely lead to you being able to collaborate with one another, have a decent level of trust, and low levels of resentment. You will assess that you have access to your partner. You will likely see your partner's behaviors or action tendencies as either helpful or at least not as an obstacle. But it is when you have the CTR – (Nasty-Nasty) interactions that things get dicey.

Common patterns marriage and family therapists (MFTs) see all the time in couples relationships will often take the form of some kind of pursuing or demanding from one partner and distancing or withdrawing from another. Dr. Sue Johnson calls these possible combinations "Demon Dialogues."[5] A pursue-pursue (sometimes called a demand-demand) tactic is what Dr. Johnson calls the "Find the Bad Guy" – where both couples attack and blame each other. Whether at home or in a therapy session, this tactic leads nowhere. This "blame-game" is something I refuse to play in my office. Why? Because finding fault is irrelevant to finding solutions. The aspect of systems theory called "circular causality" that we reviewed in chapter four tells me as a therapist that usually both parties have some portion of responsibility for the scenario that they are in. Stopping their cycle is far more important than figuring out "who started it." When couples are blaming each other in a "Find the Bad Guy" mode I know they are in the competing style of conflict resolution. They are being highly assertive with little to no cooperation. That's not where I want

THE TRAIL TO LOVE

them to be, and spending time and energy finding the bad guy only reinforces their polarized positions. I know that to change things around I have to get them to maintain their assertiveness (but often in a more gentle approach) and increase their cooperation. I have to find a way to get them to increase their trust and reduce their resentment through repair attempts to get the CTR cycle converted to positive and jumpstart the system in a healthier direction.

The more common tactic is a pursuer-distancer or demand-withdraw pattern – What Dr. Johnson calls the "Protest Polka."[6] Here one partner pursues the other demanding that their loved one meet some need of theirs. In true competing style, the first partner is focused on themselves and their needs. The second partner distances or withdraws employing either an avoiding or accommodating style of conflict resolution. They don't like the conflict and drama so they either avoid or acquiesce. The more the pursuer pursues, the more the distancer distances. Like a choreographed dance step, the couple responds to each other in synch. The one taking the lead moving in and the other one backing away in equal proportion to their partner's advance. Occasionally, the distancer may change their dance step. They may switch to a topic where they can more easily advance or demand, thus throwing their partner off guard and causing them to retreat. The protest polka of pursuer-distancer reverses course as the partners switch roles. Back and forth they go circling around the same "extreme three" moves of competing, accommodating, and avoiding.

A third common approach is a withdraw-withdraw tactic or what Dr. Johnson calls the "Freeze and Flee"[7] step. Here, both of the couples keenly feel threat from the other partner and are either in the "freeze" mode of the red portion of the Polyvagal Chart or the "flight" mode of the yellow portion of Porges' model. Neither feel safe to engage the other. Their trust and regard are low so they can't muster the necessary effort to collaborate and begin to attach. They are both stuck in the avoiding style of conflict resolution.

The question often comes, "Why do people pursue and why do others distance or withdraw?" I believe pursuers pursue out of anxiety or insecurity. They want to engage emotionally and relationally, but they aren't reading their partner's cues that their pursuit is overwhelming their partner. In their self-focus, they can't see their partner's needs. The pursuer sees their partner's lack of engagement (if they are paired with a partner that is withdrawing) or their partner's demands (if they are paired with someone that is pursuing or demanding) as a threat. So, they respond to the threat by "fighting" for their relationship or taking-action to allay their fears. People who withdraw are in protection mode. They see a threat in their partner's actions (either their partner's pursuit or withdrawal) and so they avoid through a freeze or flee strategy. I often tell clients, "Don't hit the panic switch." These pursuer-distancer patterns stem from anxiety and insecurity, so we need to allay the source of the anxiety and insecurity through this emotionally savvy attachment process. In therapy, I generally find it helpful to work with the pursuer first to get them to back away and reset the homeostasis equilibrium of the couple's relationship. They tend to be more capable of change than the withdrawer, who is often immobilized by the fear or threat level.

It is very crucial to view your partner's motivations behind their action tendencies (whether they are pursuing or withdrawing) as a logical (and often physiological) response to a perceived threat. Have you ever noticed that during a heated argument you are likely to give yourself the benefit of the doubt, but see your partner's viewpoint in the worst possible light? That's because human beings are horrible at being fair and unbiased. One cognitive moral development researcher, Dr. Jonathan Haidt, argues that human brains are hardwired to see more "my-side" points to an argument than "other-side" points to an argument.[8] When we perceive physical or emotional threats and enter the yellow or red portions of the Polyvagal Chart, we naturally become self-focused, self-protective, and therefore self-biased. Only when we change our misperceptions or misattributions to more accurately include our partner's motivations from their perspective can we truly see what is happening and convert the cycle between each other to a positive one through moving to collaboration rather than compromising or the "extreme three." Collaboration is a key to reducing misperceptions and misattributions. When we do use collaboration to increase trust, reduce resentment, and begin at the pathway of the TRAIL to Love, we will be well on our way to a secure attachment. Changing misperceptions to accurate perceptions and misattributions to attributions that are inclusive of our partner's perspective is how we can deepen our understanding of one another and of the interaction process of the system. Thus, we need to utilize the safety and social engagement in the trust and regard stages to "stay in the green" and have more open and accurate perceptions.

So, just what does drive or motivate our partner? The answer is emotions and attachment needs. Though we may want to see ourselves as primarily rational beings, the research literature tells quite a different story. Dr. Jonathan Haidt, a Professor of Ethical Leadership at New York University, is a social psychologist who has studied how people think and feel about moral arguments. His research has conclusively demonstrated people tend to be driven by their emotions and then afterward make up a cognitive rationale to justify their intuitively reached judgements and positions.[9] So, learning to look deeply at your own and your partners emotions before reaching a conclusion – in other words suspending your judgment about what is driving your and your partner's action tendencies and motivations until you understand their emotions and attachment needs – is a very wise course of action. The less reactive and more open we are to discussing and hearing things out from a non-defensive position, the more accurate our perception – the story we tell ourselves about why things are happening the way they are happening – will be. In other words, the behavioral explanations (actions by you and your partner) and the cognitive explanations (the thoughts and perceptions you have about why you and your partner are behaving a certain way) about your relationship are very incomplete without truly understanding the emotions and the attachment needs that drive those emotions. Learning to be patient and listen to the emotional content of your partner's needs is crucial.

We typically speak of primary and secondary emotions as we seek to understand these interactions by couples. Primary emotions tend to be the deep, vulnerable feelings that we are afraid to verbalize to our partner (and sometimes to ourselves). We may or may not be aware of them as we go through life day by day. Secondary emotions are the less vulnerable feelings – ones we don't mind if others see in us and that we are readily aware of. The primary emotions drive the secondary emotions. So, for example, if you feel excluded by a friend the primary emotions of loneliness or rejection may lead to a secondary emotion like anger or resentment.

Though it doesn't always work this way, most of the time I see couples whose secondary emotions are defensive and protective in nature. They often use the secondary emotions to cover or protect their primary emotions from being seen by others. That's because the primary emotions can be so vulnerable – much more vulnerable than the levels of vulnerability we saw with trust and regard stages. That's why in the CAST version of the Couple's Cycle Diagram (Figure 11), there is a dashed line cutting across the diagram. The items above the line such as action tendencies, (Mis)perceptions/attributions, and secondary emotions are the things we typically see in our partner and allow to be seen in ourselves. The items below the line (primary emotions and deep attachment needs) are items we either are not aware of or are protecting that we don't allow others to see. The development of healthy, secure attachments in a couple occurs at these vulnerable levels of primary emotions and deep attachment needs. By focusing on understanding and experiencing those items in ourselves and in our partners, we can begin to connect and feel close to one another in a healthy, attached relationship.

Like peeling the layers of an onion, your CAST trained therapist will assist you to move from the behavioral action tendency level to the cognitive perception level while also exploring your patterned cycles (including your version of pursuer-distancer patterns). They will strive to help you use the concept of collaboration to convert your cycles to positive Collaboration-Trust-Resentment cycles within and between the two of you. From there your therapist should explore your secondary and primary emotions. They will also explore your deep attachment needs. These needs may arise from early childhood experiences or things that have happened recently in your significant relationships – including your marriage(s) or romantic partnership(s) – past and present. All humans have the need to feel safe and secure, to feel that important people in their life care for them, and that they are cherished and valued. Experiences, feelings, thoughts, or behaviors that impair a secure attachment will be explored by your therapist and between you and your partner in your counseling sessions.

HOMEWORK – Chapter 3: Attachment History Assignment

Take a moment to reflect on Figure 3 (earlier in this chapter). You will be asked to work with your therapist at the next session (and possibly more than one session) to outline an Attachment History assignment. In preparation for your next therapy session, each of you write down or type out the answers to the following questions[10] on a separate paper that you will take to your therapist:

Part A: Childhood Attachment History

1. In your childhood, who did you turn to when you needed to be soothed or comforted?
2. What types of things did that person do to soothe or comfort you?
3. Did you feel that the person you turned to for comfort was dependable, available, and cared about your well-being? If so, how did you know you could trust them and rely on them? If not, what did they do to make you feel they were unreliable or untrustworthy?
4. When were you most likely to be soothed or comforted by them? When were you least likely to be soothed or comforted by them?
5. How did you communicate or let them know that you were seeking their comfort, soothing, or assistance with your needs?
6. Were there ever times when this person was not available to

comfort or soothe you? What was different about those times when you were not comforted or they were not available to comfort you and you had to turn to someone else?
7. Did you ever have to comfort yourself or self-soothe because no one was available to comfort or soothe you?
8. Was there ever a time or times when you felt betrayed, rejected, or purposefully ignored by the person or persons you usually turned to for comfort and soothing?
9. Did you ever seek comfort from things other than people, such as alcohol, drugs, sex, gambling, excessive shopping, or other potentially addicting habits or behaviors?
10. Did you have any significant traumatic experiences in childhood that may affect how you relate to people now?
11. How would you summarize your life's lessons from childhood about attachment and connection to significant others in your life?

Part B: Adult Romantic Attachment History

1. As an adult, did you have any significant prior relationships before your current marriage or partnership? If so, what were those relationships like?
2. In prior relationships, what were your attachment patterns like – secure, anxious, avoidant, or something else?
3. Were there any instances that were traumatic, abusive, or deeply disheartening and painful experiences in that prior relationship?
4. In your current relationship, how would you characterize your attachment relationship patterns – secure, anxious, avoidant, or something else?
5. Have there been any instances that were traumatic, abusive, or deeply disheartening and painful experiences in your current relationship?

6. How do you seek for comfort or soothing from your current partner?
7. What are the three most common ways you make a "bid for attention or connection" with your current spouse or partner?
8. In most circumstances, do you tend to pursue and demand or are you more likely to distance and withdraw yourself? What is your partner's typical tactic regarding pursuing or distancing?
9. What stories or perceptions do you tend to tell yourself about why your current spouse or partner tends to act the way they do? What do you attribute their most irksome or bothersome behavior to in your relationship?
10. What stories or perceptions do your tend to tell yourself about your own behaviors and actions? Do you ever perceive that you sometimes bias your perceptions to see yourself in the best light possible and perhaps see your spouse's behaviors in a critical or negative way?
11. What primary emotions can you identify about your partner or spouse? (Ask your therapist for a feelings chart or feelings wheel if you have difficulty in this portion of the assignment). Can you link one or two primary (vulnerable) emotions with any secondary (defensive) emotions? Where do you think those feelings stem from?
12. What is your deepest unmet attachment need or needs? To feel safe, secure, connected, not ever abandoned, cherished, and/or valued?

Recommended Readings

- Stan Tatkin (2011). *Wired for Love: How Understanding Your Partner's Brain and Attachment Style Can Help You Defuse Conflict and Build a Secure Relationship.* Oakland, CA: New Harbinger Publications, Inc.
- Sue Johnson (2019). *Attachment Theory in Practice:*

Emotionally Focused Therapy (EFT) with Individuals, Couples, and Families. New York, NY: Guilford Press.
- Amir Levine and Rachel Heller (2011). *Attached: The New Science of Adult Attachment and How It Can Help You Find – and Keep – Love.* New York, NY: TarcherPerigee.

CHAPTER FOUR - INTIMACY

*I*ntimacy. What first comes to your mind when you hear that word? Desire, sex, passion? Emotional closeness and connection? Yes, those are all parts of intimacy, but intimacy is so much more. Intimacy has many dimensions – emotional, physical (including sexual), intellectual, social, and spiritual. Intimacy involves knowing your partner and yourself totally. It is a more vulnerable, deep gift of sharing and receiving with the utmost care and consideration for one another. It builds on the trust, regard, and attachment that comes from "being there" for each other in predictable, consistent ways.

In a previous book,[1] I defined intimacy in the following way:

"Intimacy is the vulnerable sharing of one's self that is received with kindness and often mutually reciprocated."

I have been using this definition of intimacy for over a decade in my classes, with clients, and in supervision of my students' clinical work. It is one of the most powerful ways to view intimacy once you break down the elemental components of that definition.

By intimacy, I mean a "total human intimacy" – not just the physical or sexual dimension of intimacy. It is important not to fragment sexual dimensions of intimacy from the other key dimensions of total intimacy. In the marriage relationship, we expect from one another the total of all the forms of intimacy possible – emotional, social, intellectual, spiritual, and sexual or physical. We want to know and connect with each other in our thoughts and feelings, our social and spiritual experiences, and physical and sexual expressions. We want to know and connect – holding nothing back – at the deepest levels of our heart, mind, body, and soul. Why? Because to be fully known and fully loved (or at least accepted) is one of the deepest human desires. But only when we are vulnerable enough to fully expose our thoughts, feelings, spiritual beliefs or impressions, social wants, and bodily desires can we be truly known by someone who can accept and love us.

Intimacy inherently involves taking the risk of vulnerability. It is risky to share our deepest thoughts and feelings and desires – to get metaphorically (and sometimes literally) naked – with our mind, heart, body, and soul. It takes courage to be so vulnerable, but without risking such vulnerability we cannot truly connect on the deepest levels. We hope that in sharing our most private thoughts, feelings, parts of our body, social relationships, and spirit that the other person will not laugh, mock, scorn, deride, or dismiss us. If we do vulnerably share ourselves, and the other person ignores, misses, dismisses, or shames us, then we will be potentially crushed by the weight of that rejection. That is why we are careful to only become truly intimate in the total way I'm talking about in *committed* relationships where we have the safety and security of trust, regard, and attachment. Commitment matters because without commitment we cannot become fully intimate in the total sense.

Keep in mind that to *share* yourself you have to *know* yourself. That is why identity is the preeminent precursor to intimacy. You simply must do the difficult identity development in the teen years before you can ever hope to be truly intimate in the adult years. Typically, identity development occurs as the teen engages in enriching social experiences that allow them to develop their interests and talents.

They develop a sense of who they are in the context of their surrounding world. When youth take the time to let social friendships and casual dating experiences – without significant physical or sexual distractions deflecting their development – happen in a natural pace, they find they are better able to engage in intimate relationships in their adult years because they are bringing a fully formed sense of self into the committed relationship.

When you vulnerably share your fully formed and deepest levels of yourself with your partner and they don't miss it, mock it, ignore it, or dismiss it – but instead, they actually receive your shared self with kindness, love, compassion, and understanding – it may seem like a miracle in some relationships. But the act of sharing one's deepest self by one partner and such sharing being received with kindness by the other followed by their own sharing back at the same deep levels is where intimacy is generated. *The human bond we call intimacy is simply that – the act of sharing, receiving, and sharing back of our most vulnerable thoughts, feelings, and yearnings of the mind, heart, body, and soul.*

But there is one more key to intimacy – that such acts of sharing, receiving, and sharing back in love and kindness happens *often*. In other words, it has to happen on a consistent, predictable basis. Because I have trusted my mind, heart, body, and soul to my spouse for years and years and she has predictably and consistently responded lovingly and kindly, as well as reciprocated and shared herself in the same vulnerable, intimate ways, I can fully trust that the next time I want to share myself with my wife – whether it be a deep thought, feeling, spiritual insight, or physical gesture of love – I can reasonably assume she will once again respond with my best interests at heart because our history in the past predicts that she will do so again in the future.

So, to summarize what my definition of intimacy has taught you thus far, intimacy is not just sexual intimacy – it is the total human connection of emotional, social, intellectual, spiritual, and physical intimacy between two people. Intimacy requires vulnerability as we share our deepest thoughts, feelings, physical gestures, social experiences, and spiritual impressions. Intimacy requires us to have completed our identity development because it is important to know ourselves before we share ourselves with someone else. Intimacy requires that our partner perceives our efforts to vulnerably share and responds with kindness, understanding, and acceptance. From the attachment stage, the partner uses the concepts of accessibility, responsiveness, and engagement to convey that they care about what we are sharing and is emotionally attuned enough to reciprocate or share back at a level that is equally vulnerable and commensurate. Moreover, intimacy requires commitment because we have to have the process of intimate bonding occur often so that we can reliably predict and depend upon our partner's consistent responses to us. Only within the safety and security of trust, regard, and attachment that comes from committed relationships can we truly find the capacity to be intimate in the fullest sense.

Take a moment and reflect on the level of intimacy you currently have with your spouse and then respond to the following questions:

Of the five dimensions of intimacy – emotional, intellectual, social, spiritual, and physical (including sexual) – which dimension is the *easiest* for you to share with your partner? Why?

Partner 1:

_____
_____
_____

Partner 2:

_____
_____
_____

Of the five dimensions of intimacy – emotional, intellectual, social, spiritual, and physical (including sexual) – which dimension is the *hardest* for you to share with your partner? Why?

Partner 1:

_____
_____
_____

. . .

Partner 2:

_____
_____
_____

How comfortable are you with being vulnerable with your partner? If there are some barriers to being comfortable with vulnerability, what are they?

Partner 1:

_____
_____
_____

Partner 2:

_____
_____
_____

When you think back to your teen years and perhaps even in early adulthood, what were the key parts of your identity (your sense of self) that you have shared exclusively with your partner? What have you held back from him or her?

Partner 1:

_____
_____
_____

Partner 2:

_____
_____
_____

What do you need to share about yourself or discover (or rediscover) about your partner to deepen your intimacy?

Partner 1:
_____
_____
_____

Partner 2:
_____
_____
_____

WHAT PREVENTS you and your partner from perceiving that one (or both) of you is trying to be more open and intimate? How can you have a more consistent experience of *often* reciprocating the open sharing of intimacy between the both of you?

Partner 1:
_____
_____
_____

Partner 2:
_____
_____
_____

SCARY CLOSE – *An Intimate Barrier*

Remember back in the previous chapter when we reviewed the role of an empathic wall that limits how much feelings from others that we let in before it overwhelms us? Some people have a very rigid, high empathic wall and don't tolerate sharing vulnerable parts of themselves with others, nor do they enjoy when others share deeply vulnerable parts with them. Much of the work therapists do around intimacy with couples isn't so much about sexual problems – it's about tolerating vulnerable thoughts and feelings that arise from intimate moments in relationships.

You see, we all engage in "impression management" tactics in one form or another. We bring to the frontstage of our lives and let people know what we want them to see, but we keep the parts we are afraid to let everyone know backstage. We are willing to perform out front on the stage only those elements of our lives we are most comfortable with. The parts of our lives we are unsure about, hesitant to reveal, or are outright ashamed of, we keep backstage where only a select few may wander. Intimacy is about inviting someone you trust and care about enough (i.e. regard) to come backstage and see all the parts of you that you just don't want to reveal to just anybody. For some people, the empathic wall blocks virtually everyone from coming back and coming to know all of them – not just the safe parts they outwardly manifest. For those types of people, any form of vulnerable intimacy is just a scary form of closeness.

Donald Miller, author of *Scary Close: Dropping the Act and Finding True Intimacy*, tells a heart-warming personal story of his process of learning to stop performing his "act," not worrying about what others think, and becoming genuine in his capacity to intimately connect. He shares this gem about being intimately known and loved:

> "… we will never feel loved until we drop the act, until we're willing to show our true selves to the people around us…Can we really trust people to love us just as we are? Nobody steps onto a stage and gets a standing ovation for being human. You have to sing or dance or something. I think that's the difference between being loved and making people clap, though. Love can't be earned, it can only be given. And it can only be exchanged by people who are completely true with each other."[2]

For most people with "intimacy issues," their primary concern is about vulnerability. It is scary to be *that* close to somebody, to have them know *everything* about you. One aspect of that scariness stems from lack of confidence in themselves. The fear may be rooted in their sense of self-worth, shame about their past, their need to avoid sensitive feelings, or anxiety about rejection. For other couples with intimacy issues, their difficulty comes from lack of confidence in their partner. Whether it is a trust issue that still isn't fully resolved, or they sense their partner's discomfort with being fully, intimately known and therefore don't want to press the issue, the disconnect of non-genuine relatedness lingers in the air like smoke after two wary parties have called a truce from a bombarding battle. Determining whether the intimacy issues stem from personal reasons or an interpersonal basis (or both), is important to resolving these concerns in your relationship.

Complete the exercises below and be prepared to discuss them with your therapist at your next session.

Are there issues relating to personal self-worth that get in the way of your ability to relate intimately with one another? If so, what are they? Where did they come from? What have you done to try to feel better about your sense of self?

PARTNER 1:
_____
_____
_____

PARTNER 2:
_____
_____
_____

ARE there things in your past or present life that you feel shame about? Are you willing to share that with your partner, therapist, or both?

Partner 1:
_____
_____
_____

Partner 2:

_____
_____
_____

ARE THERE STILL ISSUES that are barriers to trust that need to be resolved with your partner? Do you need help from your therapist in being able to address those issues further?

Partner 1:

_____
_____
_____

Partner 2:

_____
_____
_____

IF YOU TEND to shy away from "deep conversations" about intimate feelings or heavy topics, is that because of your lack of tolerance for those discussions or because of your partner's reticence to do so?

Partner 1:

_____
_____
_____

Partner 2:

_____
_____
_____

Sexual Intimacy

Although sexual intimacy is covered more extensively in the next workbook in Task 9, we need to begin to address it here. Sexual intimacy, along with all of the dimensions of intimacy, is important to your relationship. Because sex is too often considered a "taboo" topic many couples come into their relationships with limited information or misinformation about sex. You and your partner may have had "the talk" with a parent or relative who may or may not have answered all of your questions when you were young. Unfortunately for some, your knowledge of sex may be limited to what you heard from friends at school, previous experiences which may or may not have been fulfilling, or from pornography which is mostly *misinformation* about human sexuality and does not depict what a loving sexual relationship with a committed partner is really like. Some people find themselves ill-equipped to talk about sex – even between themselves as a couple. Collaboration as a team in this dimension of intimacy in your lives is extremely crucial. Learning to talk about your sexual intimacy with one another and evaluate what sex means to you both is important. Having such intimate and vulnerable conversations about what is working and not working in your sexual dimension of your relationship is important to improving that vital aspect of your lives together.

WHAT WERE some of the sources you used to learn about sex when you were young?
Partner 1:
_____
_____
_____
Partner 2:
_____
_____
_____

WHAT PARTS of your sexual relationship are working well in your relationship?

. . .

Partner 1:

_____
_____
_____

Partner 2:

_____
_____
_____

What are areas of your sexual intimacy life together that you would like to work to improve?

Partner 1:

_____
_____
_____

Partner 2:

_____
_____
_____

Homework – Chapter 4: Intimacy Questions

Play a game of Intimacy Questions with your partner or spouse. They can be ones you come up with or ones from sources from the internet or various available apps. Plan to spend at least an hour or more playing the game. Be sure to take turns and go back and forth in your discussions between you. Try to give lengthened, deep answers and take time to explore each other's answers. Delight in the "joy of rediscovering" your partner.

Suggested apps for phones and tablets:

- Card Decks by The Gottman Institute
- Love Nudge from Gary Chapman's *The 5 Love Languages*
- 50 First Date Questions
- Many more available in your app store

Additionally, a few websites are provided below:

- https://www.couplesinstitute.com/play-twenty-questions-with-your-partner/
- https://faithfullyplanted.com/date-night-questions-for-couples/
- https://www.scienceofpeople.com/deep-questions/

Recommended Readings

- Weir, Kyle N. (2016). *Intimacy, Identity, and Ice Cream: Teaching Teens and Young Adults to Live the Law of Chastity.* Springville, UT: Cedar Fort Publishing.
- Donald Miller (2014). *Scary Close: Dropping the Act and Finding True Intimacy.* Nashville, TN: Nelson Books

CHAPTER FIVE - LOVE

In my family therapy theories class, a course for students beginning their first semester studying to be marriage and family therapists, I ask them how we know certain things in academics. I take the position that I'm an anthropologist from Mars or some other planet that knows nothing or very little about humans here on earth. I start out with a simple question about history, "How do you know about Abraham Lincoln?" That's the easy question. Their responses usually tell me about stories in books, speeches he wrote, statues of him, and even photographs of the man. They usually get on a roll and warm up to answering questions through this process. Then I ask them the harder question, "How do you know when you're in love?" Blank stares are the first response, and I can almost hear the crickets chirping through the window from the silence in the room. Because they feel awkward in silence, someone starts to stammer something like, "I don't know. You just feel it." I purposely confuse the word "feeling," which they meant as an emotion, for a bodily sensation and start asking where in their body they feel it. I continue to play dumb for a while to try to get them really pondering on how something so experiential as "being in love" is really, really hard to put into words.

After a few more inarticulate responses, I decide to cajole them a little, "Come on, you are all studying to be marriage and family therapists. From what I hear, love is a pretty important part of marriage and family life. You are the experts here. What is love?" Eventually some brave soul starts to speak, "You feel happy when you are with the person you love and sad and start to miss them when you aren't with them." A few more responses similar to that will come along until someone asks something like, "Dr. Weir, what kind of love are you asking about? There're different kinds. Some love is for your romantic partner, some for your kids, others for your friends or pets, and so on." The lecture goes on from there about epistemology – the study of how we know what we know.

The question of love, what it is, what types of love there are, how we show it, do we "fall" into it or is it a choice to love, and how to keep it once we've found it is as hard for the "experts" to define as my students first experience in my class, but that hasn't stopped philosophers, poets, musicians, essayists, playwrights, screenwriters, and yes – even marriage and family therapists – from trying to define it, describe it, and debate it for centuries.

In a familial sense, love is an emotion – one of the most powerful emotions known in human existence – that encompasses a desire to bind our lives with another, be that a spouse, child, parent, sibling, or other relative. But there are many facets and developmental stages to love. My own father, a retired elementary school teacher who had been married to my mother for nearly sixty years before his passing, once told me that "love is like a diamond – each side or cut (what jewelers call a "facet") of the diamond is a different type of love." This metaphor of "love is like a diamond" with many "facets" can be very instructive as we will see in this chapter. Just like a diamond begins as carbon – the basic element of life – and is transformed developmentally over time through a series of intense pressures and heat, love is an essential element for our lives, transforms over time, and requires withstanding the pressures and heat of life's challenges to become a thing of beauty. Raw diamonds do not emerge from the earth's mantle in a smooth-cut, polished form, but instead require a human hand to intentionally, cut, shape, and polish through great work and effort to become a precious, valuable, item of beauty. So, too, the love of long-term marriages and other romantic relationships requires both partners to work over long periods of time with intentionality, vision, effort, determination, and care so that the facets of their love shine brightly. Typically, the more facets a diamond has, the more people value its brilliance. But diamond experts tell us it is not just the number of facets a diamond has that makes it shine brightly, it is the high number of well-proportioned and symmetrical cuts of each facets that leads to the diamond's "fire, brilliance, and scintillation."[1] For loving romantic relationships, just having worked at loving each other from different angles or attempts over a lot of years won't always produce the brilliant love you desire. Instead, you have to work in collaborative proportion to one another using the principles outlined in these workbooks (and in other writings and books which I have recommended as further readings) to get the most joy and happiness in your loving relationships. Fortunately, you have the tools and stages of the TRAIL to Love to form the loving marriage or partnership that you desire.

To fully understand what love is, we have to understand what love is not. Love is not limerence. *Limerence* is a term therapists and researchers of marriage and family life use to describe what most people call "falling in love." Limerence is the euphoria that comes from the novelty of new relationships and usually only lasts for about two years or less in these new relationships (sometimes slightly longer if an illicit, secret affair is the object of one's devotions). Limerence is a state of attraction and infatuation (sometimes to the point of obsession) that gives rise to powerful feelings of desire, interest, and elation found in the bliss of emerging relationships. The phrase "falling in love" is a misnomer. It should be called "falling in limerence" because these early feelings are not "real love" – they are the precursor to "real love." Real love begins when and where the limerence wears off. When the novelty of the relationship with its blindness to a partner's faults starts to give way to the stark realities of the relational situation – both good and bad – and are plainly viewed, that's where the real work of building and sustaining "real love" can begin. Don't be surprised by how often the word "work" comes up in the process of building true love. Remember, collaboration means "co-laboring" or "working together" to get the love you both desire. It is when limerence ends that the work of love can begin, but the fruits of those labors can eventually be so sweet that all the effort is deemed worth it by you and your partner.

Real love requires at least these three components: "conscious choice," "effort" or collaborative work, and being "genuinely interested in fostering the personal growth of the other person."[2] After limerence has faded, we have to make a conscious choice to choose to love our spouse or partner. Love is a decision we truly make. We make that decision to love in the hard times when things aren't going the way we want, when we feel hope ebbing away, and when we determine to maintain commitments that we have made to one another in previous times that seemed happier. We also decide to love when things are ho-hum, not bad but a little boring, or just average and we know that we need to nurture our love by conscious actions that will keep love moving in the right direction. And yes, we also decide to love our partners, when things are going great – when we feel the love renewed and reciprocated – because we strive to deepen and expand an already great relationship into something even greater. Love is something we can decide to show and do and feel no matter how good or bad things are going. We can always consciously choose or decide to love, and then back up that decision through our collaborative efforts and actions.

After the conscious choice to love, comes the effort. The principal principle of CAST is collaboration. But working on a loving marriage or partnership need not be drudgery. Yes, collaboration implies that you will be tired sometimes. You will have to sacrifice something good for something better from time to time. And while it is always important to have limits or boundaries so that you aren't always on the point of exhaustion, you must realize that great romantic relationships require great amounts of effort. There is no shortcut to happy marriages around the principle of work. You must go through work.

You can't avoid or circumnavigate that principle. But remember working on something you are really passionate about can be a reward of its own. Many people "love to work" on something they really believe in. You have to adjust your mindset to "love to work on the work of love" in order to make this collaborative portion of love a joyful process. Remember, there are typically small rewards along the way to keep you motivated to keep working. You will find moments where you get the "joy of rediscovering" your love for your spouse like "two strangers (who) learn to fall in love again."[3] But unlike limerence, the rekindled loving feelings can last and deepen.

Finally, real love is genuinely interested in the growth of one another. Real love is not selfish. The kindness and compassion you show your partner flows genuinely out of your deep desire that they grow into their best self. Dr. Gary Chapman, author of the popular book *The Five Love Languages*, writes that real love is the type of love that is "emotional in nature but not obsessional. It involves an act of will and requires discipline, and it recognizes the need for personal growth."[4]

Let me illustrate this principle of love involving personal growth with personal example. When Allison and I first got engaged, she had a full ride scholarship to an Ivy League school in the eastern United States to get her master's degree in social work. I was still completing my undergraduate work at USC in Los Angeles. She cared so much about my personal growth and our future family that she passed up the opportunity to go to graduate school at that time. This wasn't done out of limerence. We'd dated for eight years by then. This was one of those hard decisions done out of pure love. I completed my undergraduate degree, masters degrees, and doctorate at USC while she worked and then stayed home with our growing family. The years have passed, the kids are all but grown and moved away starting their own lives, and I am teaching at Fresno State. Using the university benefits from my position as a professor, Allison is now studying to get her graduate degree in counseling at Fresno State. As I write this, she is studying for an exam. I am so grateful that I can do something to allow her to pursue her personal growth and educational goals after the great sacrifice she made for me. No, her degree will not be an "Ivy League" degree, some may counter, but that's not the point. The point is that we learned to make mutual decisions that benefits our family and still show great interest in the mutual growth and personal development of one another. If you ask her (and I have), she doesn't regret her decision for one minute. She is happy that her marriage and family have flourished through the choices she made and that she is still blessed with the opportunity to learn and then work in a field that she loves. Love is often accumulated by the choices we make over the years.

Take a moment to reflect on the three parts of real love – the conscious decision to love, collaborative effort or work, and unselfish interest in your partner's growth. On a scale of 1 to 10 with 10 being the highest, where would you rank your commitment to these key components of love? (Circle the Number)

Partner 1
Conscious Decision_____ 1 2 3 4 5 6 7 8 9 10
Collaborative Work _____ 1 2 3 4 5 6 7 8 9 10
Partner's Growth _____1 2 3 4 5 6 7 8 9 10

Partner 2
Conscious Decision_____ 1 2 3 4 5 6 7 8 9 10
Collaborative Work _____ 1 2 3 4 5 6 7 8 9 10
Partner's Growth _____1 2 3 4 5 6 7 8 9 10

WHY DO you believe you ranked each component where you did and what would it take to increase your score on each area?

PARTNER 1:
_____
_____
_____

Partner 2:

_____
_____
_____

TYPES OF LOVE

So, if love is something we choose, work for, and unselfishly grow, why are there different "types" of love and how do we show or express love in a variety of ways? The ancient Greek philosophers recognized that there is one style of love for a romantic partner, another for children or other relatives, and yet another for companions or friends. In fact, the Greek names for the types of love are often the roots words for English words about the different types of love. For example, the Greeks called the sexual form of desire or love *Eros* which we now call erotic love. The Greek *Agape* represented a selfless or altruistic love and *Storge* represented a love for family members such as parent-child or other relative relationships. *Philia* represented the friendship or companionship form of love. These, and other, Greek terms for love scratched the surface of helping us know what love is, but when it comes to love in romantic relationships, we need to delve deeper to truly understand what love in a spousal-partnership sense means.

Dr. Robert Sternberg, a Professor of Human Development at Cornell University, developed what he calls a "triangular theory of love."[5] He believes that love rests on three key elements: Intimacy, Passion, and Commitment. While his definition of intimacy is slightly different than the one I presented in this workbook, Sternberg's definition of intimacy seems to combine elements of Trust, Regard, Attachment, and Intimacy from the TRAIL to Love in his model. For Sternberg, intimacy is the "closeness, connectedness, and bondedness in loving relationships."[6] Passion is defined by Sternberg as the drive that leads to "romance, physical attraction, sexual consummation, and related phenomenon in loving relationships."[7] Finally, commitment refers to the decision that one loves the other and their commitment to maintain that love either in the short-term or long-term.[8] When you look at these three concepts of love – intimacy, passion, and commitment – as the vertices of a triangle and then examine how they may interact with one another, there are eight possible combinations of types or forms of love that result depending on the varying amounts of intimacy, passion, and commitment levels in the relationship: non-love, liking, empty, infatuation, romantic, companionate, fatuous, and consummate.

In Sternberg's model non-love means there is no amount of intimacy, passion, or commitment in a relationship. Liking emphasizes only intimacy with no passion or commitment. Empty love is all commitment with no passion or intimacy. Infatuation is all passion with no intimacy or commitment. Romantic love combines intimacy and passion only. Companionate love is only intimacy and commitment, but lacks passion. Fatuous love (meaning a silly or pointless form of love) combines passion and commitment. Consummate love combines all three components and is typically the goal most marriages and long-term loving partnerships are striving for. These forms of love that result from Sternberg's triangular theory of love are outlined in Figure 4.[9]

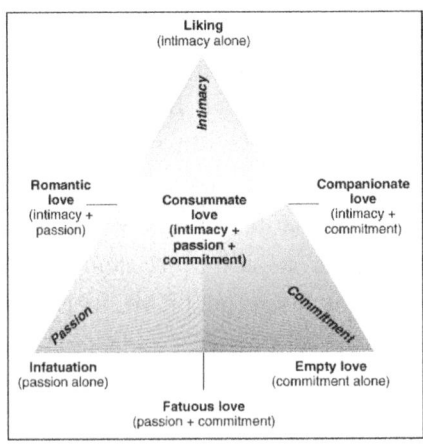

Figure 4. Sternberg's Triangular Theory of Love

As a couple, be prepared to have a conversation with one another and with your therapist about the type of love you feel for each other now and the type of love you hope to develop in your relationship. Though most couples "want it all" in the form of "consummate love," you and your partner may have something else in mind.

EXPRESSING *Love*

As mentioned previously in this chapter, love is a powerful emotion. But loving emotions unexpressed are missed opportunities to connect. For love to be shared between the two of you, the feelings of love need to be communicated and received in ways both partners understand, accept, and appreciate. Dr. Gary Chapman's book, *The Five Love Languages,* may hold the key to help you learn how to effectively give and receive love to one another. He posits five ways or "languages" for how we express and receive love in our relationships. These five love languages are:

1. Words of Affirmation
2. Quality Time
3. Receiving Gifts
4. Acts of Service
5. Physical Touch.

In reality, most people enjoy all five love languages to some degree, but there is usually one or two ways that we most feel loved. Maybe you really like it when your partner praises you, tells you he or she loves you, and comments positively about your traits and attributes (words of affirmation). For others, they most feel loved when they slow down and take the time to spend quality time together and be there for each other (quality time). Still others find that love is most effectively expressed to them through thoughtful, considerate gifts that show how much their partner cares for them (receiving gifts).

Others may not be great at words or gift-giving, but they show the people they love just how much they love them by how they serve them, do kind things for them, and help out in thoughtful, needed ways (acts of service). Finally, some people enjoy the other four expressions of love, but what really, really helps them feel loved is when they are hugged, held, kissed, and touched in loving gestures (physical touch).

Dr. Chapman's main point is that sometimes couples are "speaking a different language" and miss out on communicating with one another how they really do love each other. You see, the problem is that we tend to give what *we* want, not what our partner wants. If I primarily feel loved through physical touch, but my wife most feels loved through acts of service, she won't interpret my hugs, kisses, and loving touches as my saying "I love you" as much as if I did the dishes, washed the car, or let her rest while I put the kids to bed. Similarly, I may not see her acts of service like packing my lunch, folding my laundry, or running an errand for me as her way of expressing her love to me as much as if she kissed, hugged or caressed me.

When we both give what we want instead of what our partner wants, we are missing opportunities to love one another in ways that will revitalize and strengthen our marriages and relationships. Instead it is crucial to understand what your partner's primary love language is and to try to express your love according to *their* primary love language, rather than your own. As you both unselfishly reciprocate by each giving the other what the partners each want, the feelings of love will grow effectively and satisfyingly. To find out what your primary love language and the primary love language of your partner is, Dr. Chapman created a quiz available online at:

HTTPS://WWW.5LOVELANGUAGES.COM/QUIZZES/. Your homework for this chapter will require you to take this free test and then apply it in your relationship.

. . .

Love is Systemic: *Repeating the TRAIL and Loving One Another All Along the Way*

Though I have written about trust, regard, attachment, intimacy, and love in this workbook like they are discreet separate things, that's not entirely accurate. Each of the stages on the TRAIL to Love are interrelated with each other and overlap in a circular and systemic way, much like the frosting on the tiered cake overflows and overlaps all of the tiers. Love is what binds and gives the cake unity. It has been mixed in each layer of the cake in small doses along each step of the TRAIL, but it culminates at the top layer.

In some ways love may be better described like a trail mix snack that you've been munching on along the way. But now you have reached the end of this leg of the journey and it is time to feast on the love you've discovered. In time, you will find that the trail isn't over. Instead the trail loops around and around, and you find that this time around the TRAIL loop to Love that Love increases the Trust, Regard, Attachment, and Intimacy growing your Love and allowing you to ascend to greater relational heights. Like a spiraling trail around a mountain, Trust, Regard, Attachment, Intimacy, and Love repeat themselves over and over along the way until you've summited to your relationship's greatest potential and desires.

To help you understand how the whole TRAIL to Love works as you repeat the process, I have provided you with a CAST Map for the TRAIL to Love (Figure 5) to conclude this workbook.

My point is that love is inherently systemic. A couple's love within their marriage or partnership involves the interactions of the cognitive, mental, emotional, and sometimes physical parts of two people recursively responding to each other, as well as forces outside their relationship. That love has been building all along the way interacting with the other stages of the TRAIL to Love. Though the first two stages emphasized collaborative principles that could be taught and the last two stages emphasized principles that had to be experientially learned, this final stage – Love – is a systemic, recursive, and dynamic force that both instigates and culminates, drives and satisfies, yearns and fulfills. Love has been present all along the way and yet it becomes something new at the summit of the trail. But unlike trails on mountain summits, this TRAIL continues to loop and build even further where physical limits end and emotional capacities continue further. Love is a renewable resource that not only never ends, but grows exponentially in proportion to the collaborative efforts we make to attach with and love one another. This multi-faceted concept of love truly is a "many-splendored thing."[10]

Homework – Chapter 5: Speaking of Love...

Start by both of you taking the couples quiz regarding your primary "love language" on Dr. Chapman's website https://www.5lovelanguages.com/quizzes/. After you have both completed the quiz and identified your primary love language, share that information with your partner. Then ask your partner for five suggestions of how you can express your love for them in *their* primary love language – five ways *they* would feel loved by you and recognize you are loving them. Be sure to follow through will all five things over a one-week period or less, if possible.

Recommended Readings

- Gary Chapman (1995). *The Five Love Languages: How to Express Heartfelt Commitment to Your Mate.* Chicago, IL: Northfield Publishing Books.
- Yerkovich, M. & Yerkovich, K. (2008). *How we love: Discover your love style, enhance your marriage.* Colorado Springs, CO: Water Brook Press.

CONTINUING THERAPY WITH COLLABORATIVE ATTACHMENT SYSTEMS THERAPY

Continue treatment with your therapist and the third workbook in the CAST model:

Twelve Collaborative Tasks for Couples: Collaborative Attachment Systems Therapy - Workbook 3 for Couples

Available on Amazon

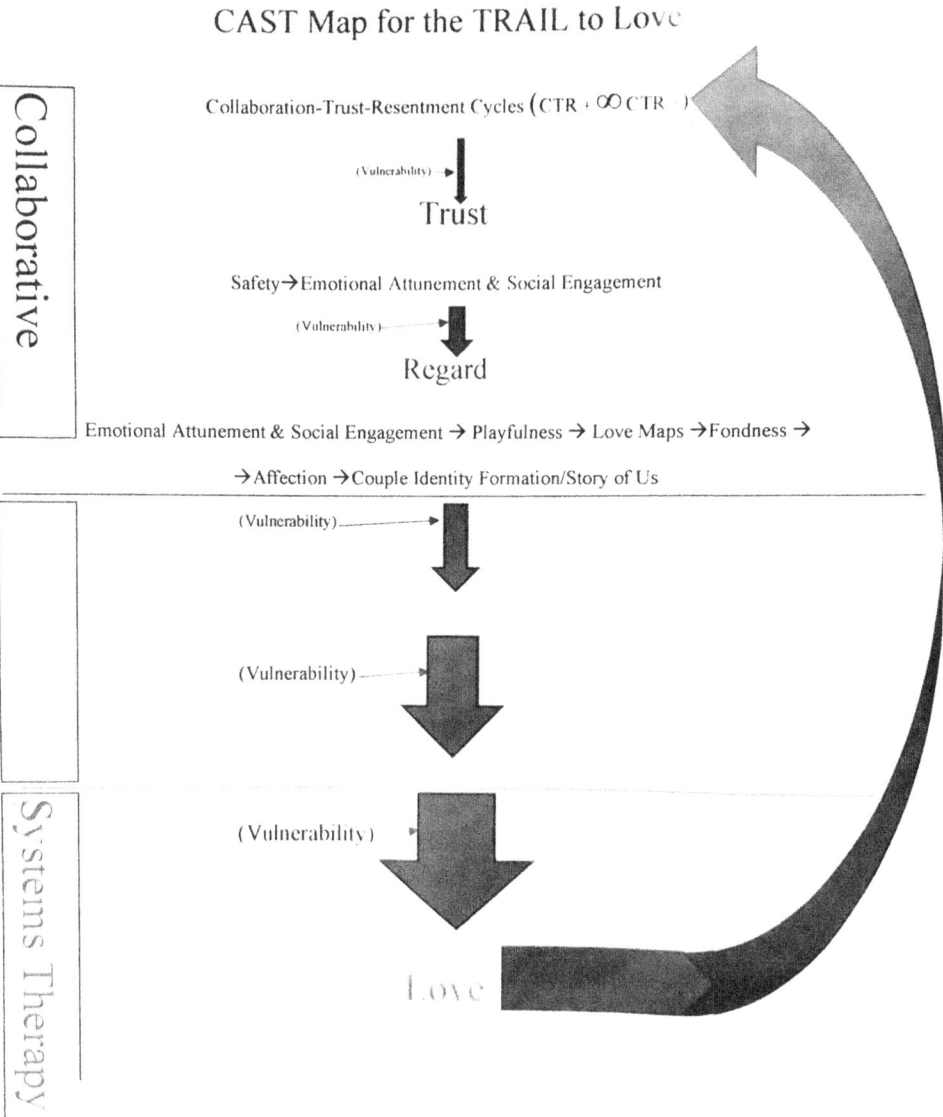

NOTES

1. CHAPTER ONE - TRUST

1. Ivan Boszormenyi-Nagy and Geraldine Spark (1984). *Invisible Loyalties*, New York, NY: Brunner-Mazel Publishers, p. xv.
2. Gottman, J.M. (2011). *The science of trust: Emotional attunement for couples.* New York, NY: W.W. Norton & Co., p. 336.
3. See the *Washington Times* news article: https://www.washingtontimes.com/news/2005/oct/04/20051004-093114-8950r/
4. Gottman, J.M. (2011). *The science of trust: Emotional attunement for couples.* New York, NY: W.W. Norton & Co., p. 336.
5. Gottman, J.M. (2011). *The science of trust: Emotional attunement for couples.* New York, NY: W.W. Norton & Co., p. 336.
6. Gottman, J.M. (2011). *The science of trust: Emotional attunement for couples.* New York, NY: W.W. Norton & Co., p. 46.
7. Gottman, J.M. (2011). *The science of trust: Emotional attunement for couples.* New York, NY: W.W. Norton & Co., p. 40.
8. Gottman, J.M. (2011). *The science of trust: Emotional attunement for couples.* New York, NY: W.W. Norton & Co., pp. 39-40.
9. Gottman, J.M. (2011). *The science of trust: Emotional attunement for couples.* New York, NY: W.W. Norton & Co., p. 46.
10. Gottman, J.M. (2011). *The science of trust: Emotional attunement for couples.* New York, NY: W.W. Norton & Co., p. 32.
11. Gottman, J.M. (2011). *The science of trust: Emotional attunement for couples.* New York, NY: W.W. Norton & Co., p. 176.
12. Gottman, J.M. (2011). *The science of trust: Emotional attunement for couples.* New York, NY: W.W. Norton & Co., p. 27.
13. Gottman, J.M. (2011). *The science of trust: Emotional attunement for couples.* New York, NY: W.W. Norton & Co., p. 334.
14. Gottman, J.M. (2011). *The science of trust: Emotional attunement for couples.* New York, NY: W.W. Norton & Co., p. 74.
15. Ivan Boszormenyi-Nagy and Geraldine Spark (1984). *Invisible Loyalties*, New York, NY: Brunner-Mazel Publishers, p. 38.
16. Ivan Boszormenyi-Nagy and Geraldine Spark (1984). *Invisible Loyalties*, New York, NY: Brunner-Mazel Publishers, p. 1.
17. Gottman, J.M. (2011). *The science of trust: Emotional attunement for couples.* New York, NY: W.W. Norton & Co., p. 68.
18. * The following 12 Crucial Steps of Rebuilding Trust are a compilation of the process outlined by Dr. John Gottman in *The Science of Trust* pp. 378-385, Drs. Gary Chapman and Jennifer Thomas in *The Five Languages of Apology*, and my own clinical experience as a marriage and family therapist and Clinical Director of LifeStar

NOTES

of the Central Valley where we facilitate disclosures by sexual addicts to their spouses/partners and then facilitate couples work.

19. See the notations after each step to see which ideas correspond to which writers:
    Turning Toward One Another (Gottman)
    Clear Admission of Faults and Secrets (Therapist-Guided Full Disclosure) (Weir)
    Expression of Genuine Remorse – The Apology (Chapman and Thomas)
    Expressing Regret – "I'm sorry" (Chapman and Thomas)
    Accepting Responsibility – "I was wrong" (Chapman and Thomas)
    Making Restitution – What can I do to make it right?" (Chapman and Thomas)
    Genuinely Repenting – "I'll try not to do that again" (Chapman and Thomas)
    Requesting Forgiveness – "Will you please forgive me?" (Chapman and Thomas)
    Transparency with Verification (Gottman)
    Process and Understand the History and Factors of the Betrayal (Gottman; Weir)
    Process Emotional Wounds from Betrayal (Gottman)
    Increase Reciprocal Cooperation (Jumpstart a CTR+ Cycle) (Gottman; Weir)
    Commit to Mutually Meeting Each Other's Needs through Collaboration (Gottman; Weir)
    Establish a High Cost for Subsequent Betrayals (Bottom Lines) (Gottman; Weir)
    Emotional Attunement is Established or Enhanced (Gottman)
    Forgiveness and Enhancing Capacity to Mentally and Emotionally Let Go (Gottman)
    Consistently Repair and Strengthen the Collaborative Story of "Us" (Gottman; Weir)
20. Gary Chapman and Jennifer Thomas (2006). *The Five Languages of Apology: How to Experience Healing in All Your Relationships*. Chicago, IL: Northfield Publishing.
21. Gary Chapman and Jennifer Thomas (2006). *The Five Languages of Apology: How to Experience Healing in All Your Relationships*. Chicago, IL: Northfield Publishing.
22. Gottman, J.M. (2011). *The science of trust: Emotional attunement for couples*. New York, NY: W.W. Norton & Co., p. 383.
23. Gottman, J.M. (2011). *The science of trust: Emotional attunement for couples*. New York, NY: W.W. Norton & Co., p. 383.
24. Gottman, J.M. (2011). *The science of trust: Emotional attunement for couples*. New York, NY: W.W. Norton & Co., p. 208.

2. CHAPTER TWO - REGARD

1. See https://www.merriam-webster.com/dictionary/regard
2. Stephen W. Porges (2011). *The Polyvagal Theory: Neurophysiological Foundations of Emotions, Attachment, Communication, and Self-Regulation*. New York, NY: W.W. Norton & Co.
3. Gottman, J.M & Silver, N. (2015). The *seven principles for making marriage work*. New York, NY: Three Rivers Press, pp. 39-41.
4. Gottman, J.M. (2011). *The science of trust: Emotional attunement for couples*. New York, NY: W.W. Norton & Co., p. 191.

5. Gottman, J.M & Silver, N. (2015). The *seven principles for making marriage work*. New York, NY: Three Rivers Press.
6. Scheibehenne, B., Mata, J., & Todd, P. M. (2011). Older but not wiser—Predicting a partner's preferences gets worse with age. Journal of Consumer Psychology, 21(2), 184-191.
7. Gottman, J.M & Silver, N. (2015). The *seven principles for making marriage work*. New York, NY: Three Rivers Press, p. 68.
8. Gottman, J.M & Silver, N. (2015). The *seven principles for making marriage work*. New York, NY: Three Rivers Press, pp. 32-39.
9. Fowler, O. S. (1875). How to establish a perfect affection. In Creative and sexual science, or, manhood, womanhood and their mutual inter-relations: Love, its laws, power, etc....as taught by phrenology. (pp. 523–583). New York, NY: Fowler & Wells, Publishers. https://doi-org.hmlproxy.lib.csufresno.edu/10.1037/12378-009
10. Don R. Catherall (2007). *Emotional safety: Viewing couples through the lens of affect.* New York, NY: Routledge, p. 14.
11. Gottman, J.M & Silver, N. (2015). The *seven principles for making marriage work*. New York, NY: Three Rivers Press, pp. 277-279.

3. CHAPTER 3 - ATTACHMENT: APPLIED

1. Gottman, J.M & Silver, N. (2015). The *seven principles for making marriage work*. New York, NY: Three Rivers Press, pp. 87-90.
2. Sue Johnson (2008). *Hold Me Tight: Seven Conversations for a Lifetime of Love*. New York, NY: Little, Brown and Company, pp. 49-50.
3. Daniel Goleman (1995). *Emotional intelligence: Why it can matter more than IQ.* New York, NY: Bantam Books.
4. See http://trieft.org/wp-content/uploads/2012/01/Cycle-Notes.jpg
5. Sue Johnson (2008). *Hold Me Tight: Seven Conversations for a Lifetime of Love*. New York, NY: Little, Brown and Company, pp. 66-67.
6. Sue Johnson (2008). *Hold Me Tight: Seven Conversations for a Lifetime of Love*. New York, NY: Little, Brown and Company, pp. 66-67.
7. Sue Johnson (2008). *Hold Me Tight: Seven Conversations for a Lifetime of Love*. New York, NY: Little, Brown and Company, pp. 66-67.
8. Jonathan Haidt (2012). *The Righteous Mind: Why Good People are Divided by Politics and Religion*. New York, NY: Vintage Books, pp. 94-95.
9. Jonathan Haidt (2012). *The Righteous Mind: Why Good People are Divided by Politics and Religion*. New York, NY: Vintage Books, chapters 2 and 3.
10. Adapted and expanded from Dr. Scott Woolley's *Attachment History Questions*.

4. CHAPTER FOUR - INTIMACY

1. Weir, Kyle N. (2016). *Intimacy, Identity, and Ice Cream: Teaching Teens and Young Adults to Live the Law of Chastity*. Springville, UT: Cedar Fort Publishing.
2. Donald Miller (2014). *Scary Close: Dropping the Act and Finding True Intimacy*. Nashville, TN: Nelson Books, pp. xv-xvi.

5. CHAPTER FIVE - LOVE

1. See https://www.capetowndiamondmuseum.org/blog/2017/05/does-a-diamond-with-more-facets-sparkle-more/
2. Gary Chapman (1995). *The Five Love Languages: How to Express Heartfelt Commitment to Your Mate.* Chicago, IL: Northfield Publishing, p. 33.
3. Journey/Jonathan Cain (1983). "Faithfully," Columbia records. See https://www.azlyrics.com/lyrics/journey/faithfully.html
4. Gary Chapman (1995). *The Five Love Languages: How to Express Heartfelt Commitment to Your Mate.* Chicago, IL: Northfield Publishing, p. 35.
5. Sternberg, R. J. (1986). A triangular theory of love. *Psychological Review*, 93, 119–135.
6. See http://www.robertjsternberg.com/love
7. See http://www.robertjsternberg.com/love
8. See http://www.robertjsternberg.com/love
9. See https://sites.psu.edu/aspsy/2015/02/15/its-all-love-roses-until-someone-gets-hurt/ for the original graphic of the triangle.
10. Fain, S., & Webster, P. F. (1955). *Love is a many-splendored thing.*

ABOUT THE AUTHOR

Kyle N. Weir, Ph.D., LMFT, is a Professor of Marriage, Family, and Child Counseling in the Counselor Education program at California State University—Fresno. He has also previously served as Chair of the Department of Counselor Education and Rehabilitation and as Coordinator of the Counselor Education program. He currently serves as the Associate Director of Fresno Family Counseling Center – a student-training clinic operated by the faculty and students of Fresno State's Marriage, Family, and Child Counseling degree serving the needs of the California Central Valley community. He primarily teaches the following courses: Couples Therapy, Family Therapy Theories, MFT Business Practices, and Advanced Practicum/Supervision courses. He received a B.S. in Public Policy and Management, an M.A. in Sociology (Organizations), a M.M.F.T. in Marital & Family Therapy, and a Ph.D. in Sociology/Marriage and Family Therapy from the University of Southern California. He is a licensed marriage and family therapist in California, was a part-time clinician at LDS Family Services, and now practices with the firm Roubicek & Thacker, Inc. He also serves as the Clinical Director of LifeSTAR of the Central Valley through Roubicek and Thacker, Inc.

He is married to Allison Brown Weir, and they have six children: Kellie, Nathan, Samantha, Joshua, Jason, and Daniel. It was through the personal adoption experiences with his children that Dr. Weir developed an academic interest in play therapy with adoptive and foster families.

He has also spent decades doing couples therapy, as well as supervising his students who engage in couples therapy. The Collaborative Attachment Systems Therapy model was developed through his academic teaching, supervision, and clinical experience with couples therapy. Dr. Weir is the author of numerous peer-reviewed journal articles and the books *Coming Out of the Adoptive Closet* (2003; University Press of America), *The Choice of a Lifetime: What You Need to Know Before Adopting* (2011; NTI Upstream), *Intimacy, Identity, and Ice Cream: Teaching Teens and Young Adults to Live the Law of Chastity* (2016; Cedar Fort Publishing); *Why Repentance Matters* (2018, Finegold Creek Press); and a forthcoming book *Saints Overcoming Scrupulosity*.

For more information visit:
    www.drkyleweir.com

For clinical appointments or questions contact:
    Kyle N. Weir, PhD, LMFT
    Roubicek and Thacker, Inc. (Private Practice)
    1879 E. Fir Ave., Suite 103, Fresno, CA 93720
    559-323-8484
    https://roubicekandthacker.com/individual-couples-family-counseling

Made in the USA
Coppell, TX
25 February 2025

46413004R00056